1789

1789

TWELVE AUTHORS EXPLORE A YEAR OF REBELLION, REVOLUTION, AND CHANGE

EDITED BY

MARC ARONSON AND
SUSAN CAMPBELL BARTOLETTI

CANDLEWICK PRESS

For Greta Thunberg and Malala Yousafzai,
two modern revolutionaries

TABLE OF

CONTENTS

INTRODUCTION

THE AGE OF REVOLUTIONS

THE FRENCH REVOLUTION, the Declaration of the Rights of Man, the European slave trade; the American Revolution, the Bill of Rights, slavery in America. When these subjects come up in a US classroom, they are treated as separate topics—one set arrives in world history, the other in American history. But, as the chapters in this book show, such a separation is entirely artificial. Events in America influenced those in Europe, the Caribbean, and Africa; events in the Pacific were shaped by those in Europe and America. Ideas, people, and money were shuttled across the world's great oceans.

In all of this movement, two great forces swelled and clashed: ideas of liberty, freedom, and rights; and the fact of enslavement and subjugation. The two opposing forces crystallized a single question—one still furiously debated today: What is a man? If, as first America and then France declared to the world, all men are equal, who is a man? Males? White males? Rich males? Christian males? Each partial answer opened a new question: If men, why not women? If Christian, could anyone become equal by converting? Who gets to be "white," and why should that matter?

The idea that there are some "rights" that every person owns simply by being a person challenged every order based on noble birth. Soon enough the idea of such rights would do battle with hierarchies of wealth, age, race, and gender. The idea of who or what has rights continues to evolve. Today some people believe that everyone has a right to economic security and that the earth—the environment—has rights, as do animals. Hundreds of years from now when someone writes about our time, what obvious violations of rights will they see?

The thinkers of the eighteenth century opened a door we are still peering through today. In this anthology, readers will encounter ideas, beliefs, and causes rippling across thousands of miles. People, events, and topics come up in a certain way in one chapter and then differently in another. You begin to feel how much was shifting in that tumultuous year of 1789. Today newscasts endlessly announce "breaking news." We hope that these chapters give readers the sense of how ideas "broke" across continents, of how immediate and alive the world was then.

We begin with France. In the opening chapter, Tanya Lee Stone sets the stage, and you're there, in the streets of Paris, amid the fishwives who lead a protest march that helps to launch a revolution. Next Karen Engelmann extends and reverses the story of 1789, showing how a contradictory Swedish king changed his country and earned the anger of noblewomen who, driven by a desire to retain their status and privileges, protested *against* expanding rights.

Amy Alznauer takes us across Europe to a battlefield where amid the bombing, we view a different side of that dramatic year—revolutions in thought—as a mathematician traces the digits of pi. Susan Campbell Bartoletti shifts our attention to a new way of examining events in Paris: through the portraits of the queen being painted by a talented female artist. Then as now, how a powerful woman presented herself—or was presented—to the public caused endless debate. Marc Aronson begins in Paris that same year, where a pregnant American teenager faces a choice that points directly to the central question in this book: the expansion of rights and freedoms, the reality and consequences of enslavement.

The central issue of slavery expands as Joyce Hansen recounts the life of a former slave whose autobiography, published in 1789, became a key tool in the abolitionist movement. Summer Edward takes us inside an arena of the global contest against slavery as she describes the journeys of a Methodist minister who brought ideas of equality to the Caribbean.

Cynthia Levinson and Sanford Levinson take us to one of the seemingly more familiar events of 1789: the passage of the US Bill of Rights in Congress. They show how keeping an eye on France helps us to view the bill, its limitations, and the ongoing conversations about its meaning in new ways. Christopher Turner's piece shines a new light on the issues around rights in North America, looking at the year 1789 and the American Revolution through the eyes of the Seneca and the other nations of the Haudenosaunee, the Six Nations.

Back in Europe, Sally M. Walker traces the findings of a British geologist whose persistent explorations prove that the earth is far older than had been believed and has evolved over millions of years. Challenging the biblical understanding of the earth's age was as revolutionary as challenging the rule of a king. Finally, linking Europe, the Pacific, and the Caribbean, Steve Sheinkin gives us the drama of a mutiny on board a British ship and leaves us with one more mystery to ponder. How much were people, spread throughout the planet, shaped by the explosion of new ideas?

In this book we present France, the United States, and the world at the tipping-point moment when so much seemed possible, and yet such profound issues remained to be faced—a bit like the possible tipping-point moment we face today.

To give some sense of how people at the time responded to these events, ideas, and conflicts, we have included four sets of contemporaneous quotations. The sources range from poems to political arguments, essays to books. The quotations are grouped based on their tone: exhilaration, abomination, inspiration, conclusions.

One of the most important quotation threads is the debate that had Thomas Paine and Mary Wollstonecraft on one side and Edmund Burke on the other. Paine loved the French Revolution of 1789 and all it promised, though he opposed its later turn to violence. Burke, who had supported the American Revolution and created the first serious and detailed plan to abolish slavery in lands controlled by the United Kingdom, thought the French Revolution was a terrible idea that would lead to ever greater violence and death until a dictator took over, which proved to be right. Burke believed that it was too dangerous to utterly disrupt the existing habits and structures of a society—no matter how flawed. Paine and Wollstonecraft disagreed with Burke; society had to be restructured. Paine argued for the rights of those abused and deprived under current conditions. Wollstonecraft furthered Paine's position but argued that women deserved the same rights and privileges of men. Versions of this debate continue to this day.

This is the second nonfiction anthology that we have created. Just as we did with our first anthology, *1968*, we invited authors to explore aspects of the year 1789 that interested them. Each chapter is an opening, a window, to people, ideas, and events that were central then and are still of interest now. We encourage readers to browse—to find which topic, which writing style, excites their curiosity, and then return again as one chapter speaks to another, and that tumultuous year of 1789 comes alive.

—Marc Aronson and Susan Campbell Bartoletti

E X H I L A

O H ! pleasant exercise of hope and joy!
   For mighty were the auxiliars which then stood
Upon our side, we who were strong in love!
Bliss was it in that dawn to be alive,
But to be young was very heaven!

. . . .

But Europe at that time was thrilled with joy,
France standing on the top of golden hours,
And human nature seeming born again.

> —*WILLIAM WORDSWORTH*, The Prelude. *The English*
> *Romantic poet visited revolutionary France in 1791.*
> *In this long autobiographical poem, Wordsworth*
> *described the enthusiasm many idealists felt for the*
> *French Revolution. For him and for many others,*
> *the idealism later turned to disillusionment.*

RATION

WE see the solemn and majestic spectacle of a Nation opening its commission, under the auspices of its Creator, to establish a government; a scene so new, and so transcendently unequalled by anything in the European world, that the name of a revolution is diminutive of its character, and it rises into a regeneration of man.

> —*THOMAS PAINE*, Rights of Man, *1791. The English-American activist deemed revolution permissible when a government does not safeguard the natural rights of its people. Fifteen years earlier, Paine had written the pamphlets that inspired American patriots to declare independence from Great Britain.*

I HAVE lived to see the rights of men better understood than ever; and nations panting for liberty, which seemed to have lost the idea of it. I have lived to see THIRTY MILLIONS of people, indignant and resolute, spurning at slavery, and demanding liberty with an irresistible voice.

> —*RICHARD PRICE*, A Discourse on the Love of Our Country, *1789. In this speech, the English minister claimed that a country is defined by its principles and its people, not its rulers or geography. He supported the French Revolution, just as he had supported the American Revolution, despite his own love for England.*

"THE FISHWIVES MAKE THE RULES"

THE OCTOBER DAYS OF THE FRENCH REVOLUTION

TANYA LEE STONE

ONE WOMAN BEAT A DRUM, signaling a storm in the streets of Paris.

Soon, hundreds of women who ran the main marketplace left their stalls for city hall that Monday morning, October 1789. They were intent on imposing their will on officials. They demanded bread. It is not known whether the officials there would not supply it or simply did not have it. Some of the women threatened to burn the officials' papers, seized weapons, and grew increasingly angry.

They knew what they had to do. The true seat of power lay twelve miles away, safely ensconced within the walls of the grand palace of Versailles. There Louis XVI and Marie Antoinette had no idea they were about to face a female force that would help change the course of the French Revolution.

→

This was no sudden awakening of women. Yes, revolutionary action had been mostly male dominated, but the females were equally furious. Frustrated, too, for the men weren't making much progress, and frankly the business of food fell squarely in the domain of the Dames des Halles. At a time when most women had few rights, a Dame—married or not—ran her own business under her own name.

The Dames indeed ruled the rowdy marketplace, running food stalls, buying and selling everything from eggs and vegetables, to fruit and flowers and fish, to cheese and butter. There was history here. Tradition. They had been the heart and soul of the Parisian food supply for five hundred years at Les Halles. In 1789 Parisians ate 78 million eggs, mainly procured through the Dames. And the Dames outnumbered bakers two to one.

Imagine a thousand or so women hawking bushels of vegetables and barrels of fish while keeping up with the neighborhood news (knowledge is power), all within the confines of a 6,000-square-meter area—only about the size of twenty tennis courts. It was a noisy, smelly place. In warm weather, flimsy parasols shaded food from the sun to keep it from spoiling too quickly. Customers wound through crowds and carts and shops, seeking out the best prices and the freshest food from their favorite Dames, who, if they were lucky, might just sell them something on credit, as poverty was widespread.

Satellite marketplaces sprang up in other parts of the city as well, and so the Dames' reach extended. They tended a complicated network of suppliers and lenders and customers, navigating both competition and camaraderie. On arriving at the marketplace early in the morning, the first task for the fishwives was to orchestrate supplies hauled in hours earlier from the countryside, dividing and distributing food into smaller lots to sell to customers. Without the Dames, there was no food supply chain in Paris. But all was not well.

As the nation struggled with major money problems, big, bold ideas were taking hold in Europe (and America). The Enlightenment— with its notions of egalitarianism, relief from oppressive rulers, and belief in brotherhood and sisterhood—had been creeping into the consciousness of the impoverished French, and its ideas were gathering steam at a rate fast enough to fuel the fire of freedom.

As grain crop production fell, the price of bread rose, and the cost was crippling to the average citizen, who had to pay two-thirds of their daily wages for their daily bread. And the quality of bread was often so bad it made people sick, with bakers being accused of hoarding grain and adding sawdust to dough to stretch their supplies.

It was not just their customers the Dames were thinking about. Many had families to feed and households to handle. "I present us," a representative Dame in a pamphlet petitioned, "as having as much right as any person, by our work, to be heard, by the sweat that we shed to support the life of the Nobility & the Clergy."

The Dames, in fact, symbolized *le peuple* and garnered much popular support in this role. They were woven into the city's very fabric. And though they were poor and often illiterate, they knew their worth. So, too, did the pamphleteers who bolstered the Dames' value in print, sometimes creating fictional spokeswomen—using their known value to the city to anchor an argument. One of these fictive Dames once explained the term "aristocrat" as those who "want all the profit without the hardship . . . like these hornets who steal honey that the bees have gone to great pains to make . . . and [they] spit on us down below."

As it stood, the French were divided into three groups, each "estate" given equal voting power. On the surface, this may sound sensible, until you consider that the First and Second Estates *combined*—the church and the nobles—made up only 2 percent of the nation's population, already enjoyed exemption from most taxes, and garnered two-thirds of any vote. This equation stripped the Third Estate—the poor and the middle class—of any real voting power at all, even though it was made up of 98 percent of the population, which mainly included peasants and farmers, but also the bourgeoisie (doctors, lawyers, wealthy merchants).

The citizens of the Third Estate were paying all the taxes and doing all the work. If nothing was challenged, the rich would grow richer; the poor, poorer.

"Our good king," as Louis XVI was oft referred, was a big part of the problem. He spared no expense for personal pleasures while enjoying a perplexing popularity among *le peuple*, who blamed the aristocracy for corrupting their learned yet ill-equipped king.

Turning a blind eye at Versailles, the king and queen continued to live in the lap of luxury, dining on fine foods to their hearts' content. Rumor even had it that Marie Antoinette was hoarding grain. And then there was the ultimate insult: a decadent banquet to welcome the troops—with more than two hundred guests! Amid the free-flowing alcohol, spirits rose, as did chants of *"Vive le roi!"* (Long live the king!).

Royal recklessness was not the only financial issue. France had spent no small sum battling Britain in the Seven Years' War and aiding the Americans in their Revolution. The solution to all of this mess? Financial reform—in the form of taxes.

An emergency meeting was arranged to address the financial crisis. But who was likely to bear the brunt of the burden? *Le peuple.* And why should they be dominated and downtrodden by the tiny percentage of their population who were living large and forcing the rest of the folks to foot the bill?

The collective anxiety and anger was about to boil over. The stage was set for an uprising.

October 5, 1789

There is a French saying: *"les poissardes font la loi"* (the fishwives make the rules). Indeed it *was* the fearsome fishwives—with their sharp knives and strong backs—who were the first to mobilize. When the marketplace opened that Monday morning, there was, as usual, little to no bread. Hungry, and tired of feeling powerless to effect legal change, the Dames des Halles took action.

The reaction that had been signaled by one woman beating a drum intensified. After the throng of women rushed city hall without satisfaction, a heavy rain began to fall. But the Dames were undeterred. Off they set for the palace in Versailles. As they marched through the middle of the Champs-Elysées, women came to meet them from every direction, armed with all manner of muskets, swords, knives, pitchforks, and pikes. Whipped up as the wind, they rounded up more women in the streets (occasionally threatening or shaming them into joining), winding their way through the city, then heading west through the countryside. They knocked on doors to recruit more and more people, adding middle-class women and men to their throngs.

The rain became relentless. All told, more than six thousand souls tromped through the streets that had turned to mud, motivated to make their needs known, bolstered by the beat of several Dames drumming, and dragging two cannon.

Two gentlemen passersby, learning of their plans, perhaps oblivious or blind to what they were witnessing, felt it their place to patronize the ladies, offering some unsolicited advice and apparent permission: "Go ahead, behave yourselves and don't be insolent to anyone."

One woman snapped back a biting reply: "We're going to Versailles; we'll bring back the Queen's head on the end of a sword."

The bread crisis was not the only pressing problem they planned to address. The Third Estate had taken matters into their own hands, forming the National Assembly. And the new National Assembly had gotten to work drafting a Declaration of the Rights of Man and of the Citizen, with the Marquis de Lafayette as principal writer (with American Thomas Jefferson, drafter of the Declaration of Independence, by his side).

The marchers likely discussed how they wanted the king to approve the Declaration and move the monarchy from the too-far-removed Versailles to the capital city. This, they probably argued, would literally and figuratively put the king where he belonged: in the heart of Paris, where change had a chance.

By nightfall, they had arrived. Things were calm, at first. According to one of the women present, Marie-Rose Barre, they "found the King's Guards lined up in three ranks before the palace. A gentleman dressed in the uniform of the King's Guards, who, she was told, was the duc de Guiche, came to ask them what they wanted of the king." After insisting their only intention was to peacefully plead for bread, a handful of women were allowed entry to speak with King Louis XVI. They climbed the marble stairs to his apartments, their already ragged clothing clinging to them from their rain-soaked journey. Standing amid the splendor, they must have been a sight.

At just seventeen, one of the marchers, Louison Chabry, "fell on her knees before the monarch, lamented that the capital had no bread, and fainted at his feet." The king gave the girl a bit of brandy and promised he would help. Louis XVI kept his word, dispersing some food, deputizing forty Dames, and sending them back to the city in royal carriages, carrying his personal message of assurance for the mayor.

Many who stayed behind distrusted this news, believing the group sent back to Paris was simply a stalling tactic, a ruse. They didn't trust that significant reform would occur and were certain the queen, Marie Antoinette, would inevitably change the king's mind.

A crush of these women therefore took a different tack. Threatening to fire on the royal guards, they crowded into the National Assembly, causing mayhem and demanding to be heard. No longer willing to wonder whether their assembly members were representing them properly, they took over the hall. They interrupted speakers, passed mock legislation, and cast uncounted votes on matters of grain circulation and distribution—the very root of the food issue at hand. One even slumped presumptuously in the president's chair.

The women took all the assembly members to task. "Do what you are asked," one said. "Don't fancy we are children you can play with; we have our arms raised." They meant business. Some even had hunting knives hooked to their skirts.

Louis XVI did not want to fight and did not want to flee (although he seems to have discussed it briefly, at the queen's urging). He did agree to sign the Declaration of the Rights of Man and of the Citizen. This document detailed human rights for all men (neither women's rights nor slavery was mentioned), including freedom of religion, freedom of speech, freedom of assembly, and separation of powers— or checks and balances.

On the point of leaving the safety and seclusion of Versailles for Paris, though, the king hesitated. His hesitation did not sit well with the crowd. And, oh, how the crowd had *swelled*. Throughout that day, thousands more had joined.

Lafayette, reluctantly leading nearly twenty thousand National Guardsmen, arrived a bit before midnight. He had tried to dissuade his men from mobilizing, but they were determined to go—with or without him, some defiant enough to level guns at their commander and threaten him with hanging if he stood in their way. And so instead, as he himself later explained, "The only thing left for me to do was to seize the movement."

His hope? Protect the king and preserve the peace. Once there, he offered reassurances to Louis XVI and Marie Antoinette, advising them to retire to their chambers for the night. It seemed things had calmed down enough to get some rest.

Many of the women had tried to retire as well, attempting to make beds out of benches in the National Assembly chambers, sprawling out wherever they could. Some took off their skirts and petticoats. They wrung the rainwater out of their garments and draped them over benches to dry. As a Lafayette aide later described, "The miserable creatures were . . . sleeping pell-mell in horrible disorder." Others sought shelter in town or camped outside the palace. The rain continued to fall.

October 6, 1789

By dawn, upward of thirty thousand well-armed French had joined the Dames and were a formidable sight. After a cold, wet night, the people wanted *in*. When an open gate was discovered, a crowd pushed its way through.

By eight a.m., there were people rushing into the courtyards and into some of the buildings. When Louis XVI learned of this development, he sent word to his troops *not* to shoot. But in the confusion, one royal guard already had, firing from a window into the chaos of the courtyard. He struck and killed a seventeen-year-old boy.

Enraged, the crowd went on attack. One man seized a guard, claiming his life in return for the boy's. Another guard's head was hacked off with an ax. The crowd was in a frothy fit.

A military commander from the province of Champagne, sleeping in a bedroom at the palace that looked out onto the Royal Court, awoke with a start to the sounds of stomping and shouting. "I jumped from my bed and ran to the window," he later wrote to his wife. He saw what had happened to the guards and heard the loud footsteps of people flooding into the building. "I really thought it was the last instant of my life."

But it was the queen's life that was really in danger. The king had already given the people a good-faith showing of much of what they asked for, sending the delegates back to Paris with bread and promises to sign the Declaration. Marie Antoinette, alas, had fallen from their favor. When that teenage boy was killed, a group went gunning for the queen, invading her bedchamber. Finding it empty, they slashed her sheets.

She had made a narrow escape just minutes before. Upon hearing the scuffle with her guardsmen as the invaders approached her apartments, the queen had just enough time to flee up a hidden staircase. The stairs went through her children's rooms and to her husband's— but when she reached the door to his chambers, it was locked!

She pounded and pounded on the door, hollering for help. Finally, her frantic voice was heard above the din, and she was let in. But the king was not there. Scared for her life, he had raced downstairs to save his queen while she was slipping through the secret passage *upstairs*. They had just missed each other. King Louis was quick to assess the situation, though, and ran back to his room, the royal couple safely reunited.

Meanwhile, Lafayette, who had gone to bed thinking things were calm, awoke and galloped back to the palace on horseback. The National Guard had managed to move the mob out of the palace, but the courtyards were still spilling over with people parading, and— as had been done at the Bastille—hiking up pikes that held those guards' severed heads.

Shouts of *"Le Roi à Paris! Le Roi à Paris!"* rang out loud and clear, ordering the king to relocate to Paris.

Only an hour or so had passed, yet despite the flurry of violence, what *le peuple* truly wanted was for their king to assure them he would abide by their wishes.

It was time for a response from Louis XVI.

Lafayette sought to calm the crowds, preparing them for the king's presence. Stepping onto a balcony above the great gathering, Lafayette said, "Messieurs, I gave my word of honor to the king that there would not be any harm done to all that belongs to His Majesty. These Messieurs are his Body Guards [royal guards], if anything would happen to them you would make me break my word of honor that I gave, I would no longer be worthy to be your leader."

With the king now standing next to Lafayette, a roar rose from the crowd: *"Vive le roi, vive le roi!"*

Louis XVI asked Lafayette to show the people a sign of unity. Bringing a royal guard onto the balcony, Lafayette removed his own tricolor cockade—representing support for the Revolution—presented it to the man, and hugged him. This sparked a chain reaction in the ranks, with royal guards ripping off their sashes and replacing them with red, white, and blue cockades offered by nearby National Guardsmen.

The crowd went crazy, with sustained shouts of "Long live the Body Guards!"

But not all were forgiven. The people demanded an appearance by the queen—alone. When Lafayette encouraged her to oblige and show her face, she cried, "What! Alone on the balcony? Haven't you heard and seen the threats that have been made against me?"

"Yes, Madame, go ahead" was his simple reply. So she stepped out onto the balcony, composed and serene—at least outwardly. Lafayette bent and kissed her hand, and her presence was immediately (and perhaps somewhat surprisingly) rewarded with a clamorous "Long live the queen!"

Louis XVI and Lafayette then announced the news: the royal family would be moving back to Paris immediately. The king's younger sister, Madame Élisabeth, described the family's procession in a letter to a friend. "At one o'clock we got into our carriages. Versailles greeted our departure with demonstrations of joy." This time, the thousands of parading people had loaves of bread—instead of heads—stuck on their staves. It took nearly seven hours, but by evening they arrived en masse.

The king and queen were taken to the Tuileries Palace, where a few French monarchs in the family had lived before. A month later, the National Assembly followed suit, moving into the largest indoor space in Paris, the covered riding ring at the Tuileries.

Of course, this is not the end of the story of the French Revolution; in fact, it is just the beginning.

But the women had *done it*—taking charge of their own fate, helping to alter the course of future events with the critical relocation of the king, shattering any illusion that the monarchy was untouchable, and standing as a symbol of the powerful will of the people. Perhaps most importantly, the women showed that the Revolution should and would include them—and that they should and would include themselves.

THE
CONTRADICTORY
KING

GUSTAV III AND THE
UNLIKELY BEGINNINGS
OF CLASS EQUALITY
IN SWEDEN

KAREN ENGELMANN

The World in Turmoil: Stockholm, Sweden, January 1789

EUROPE in the opening days of 1789 was seething with discontent and unrest. Old structures of power were in question as the ideas of the Enlightenment—about reason, science, and individual liberty—took hold. Common people demanded a more democratic government and often did so violently. England was still mourning the 1783 loss of the American colonies; Holland's William V, Prince of Orange, barely hung on after fleeing the Hague in 1785 pursued by citizens intent on representation; and in late 1788, King Louis XVI of France was forced to call the first meeting of the Estates General since 1614. King Gustav III of Sweden watched as these tumultuous events threatened the world order he was born into and raised to uphold and defend—the monarchy—and took action to consolidate his power.

His stage: a meeting of the Riksdag (Swedish parliament) in January 1789.

His adversaries: members of the Riksdag representing the First Estate—the nobles.

His champions: the three estates of the commoners—the clergy, burghers, and peasants—along with the citizens of Stockholm.

His means: the Act of Unity and Security—a coup and revolution in one. A coup because it gave the king enormous power. A revolution because the legislation contained the seeds of equality and democracy. A contradiction, and yet true.

The Riksdag of late eighteenth-century Sweden was a representative body similar to Congress in the United States, but seats were based on social class. Only men could participate, and four groups—called estates—were represented.

The aristocracy, or House of Nobles, was the First Estate. Membership in this group was dependent on title, which could be inherited or bestowed by the king. The nobles represented only 1 percent of the population but held the vast majority of land and wealth and were the largest and most powerful estate with 950 members.

The First Estate held a seventeen-year grudge against the king. In 1772 the newly crowned Gustav (just twenty-five years old) forced a new constitution, taking back power from the nobles. For fifty-two years, the government had been controlled by the Riksdag. Since the nobility held two-thirds of the votes, Sweden functioned as an aristocratic democracy with the king a mere figurehead living in a very nice house. Gustav's parents (especially his mother) fought their entire lives to restore control to the monarchy, and shortly after his coronation, Gustav made his mother proud by declaring the country a constitutional monarchy: the ruler was head of state, sharing powers of taxation, allocation of funds, and engagement of the nation's army and navy with the Riksdag. Outraged nobles formed the Patriots, a group determined to overthrow the king.

From 1772 on, there were whispers and plots about deposing Gustav by any means necessary (including kidnapping and assassination), then replacing him with his younger brother Duke Karl. Karl was all in favor of this and went so far as secretly having himself anointed king in 1784 when Gustav was traveling in Italy. Karl and the Patriots were eventually joined by Gustav's youngest brother, Fredrik Adolf; his sister, Sofia Albertina; and his queen, Sofia Magdalena, a Danish princess. (They were engaged as a political strategy when she was five and married when she was nineteen. They were a miserable couple.) The nobility and royal family all enjoyed the king's largesse, money, and titles, but basically wanted him dead.

Despite all this plotting and intrigue, King Gustav kept his throne *and* his love and admiration for the aristocracy—at least the idea of it. He felt they were the highest and best of humanity, descendants of legendary knights, educated, honorable, and refined. He had especially high regard for the noble ladies who brought beauty, grace, and refinement to the Swedish court, which had never been so brilliant. Or so dangerous. Educated and ambitious, noblewomen exercised considerable power behind the scenes in this strict patriarchal society. Gustav referred to these aristocratic women as his Fifth Estate.

The other three estates were lumped together as commoners. They held a combined total of 342 seats (about one-third of the Riksdag) while representing 99 percent of the populace. The Second

Estate was the clergy. Despite the small number of representatives (52), they were a powerful group that played an important role in everyday life. The church was a state institution controlled by the king, and citizens were obliged to belong, give money annually, and attend services. The Third Estate was the burghers—established merchants, craftsmen, and business owners from the cities and towns. They were powerful citizens and represented important financial and trade interests. They sent 112 representatives. The Fourth Estate was the peasants (officially called the "Honorable Estate")—settled farmers, miners, and woodsmen. They held 178 seats.

The king praised the commoners' valor and patriotism, their loyalty and love, but he did not like their company. He never ate at the same table with a commoner in his life. They were his responsibility, not his equals. Despite this, the majority of common people loved and admired Gustav from the time he was crowned king as a dashing twenty-five-year-old. He was the first Swedish-born king in over fifty years. (His grandfather, father, and mother were from parts of what is now Germany.) He spoke the native language! (His parents spoke German. The language of court throughout Europe was French.) He was educated and refined. Gustav had a flair for the dramatic and created public spectacles in Stockholm with pageantry, food, and drink. He freely walked the streets and liked being known as the first citizen among his citizens (as long as he didn't need to mingle). Shortly after his coronation, Gustav declared that every Monday, Tuesday, and Wednesday afternoon between four and five o'clock, anyone could come to the palace to speak with him on any topic—often involving money. (The event was called the Beggar's Audience.) The people saw him as one of their own, and while there was a free press and open discussion of Enlightenment and even revolutionary ideas, it did not shake the commoners' loyalty to their king.

Gustav was counting on their support in the upcoming Riksdag of 1789. His business was urgent: maintain Sweden's sovereignty against foreign invasion. The threat was real. Gustav's dear cousin, Empress Catherine the Great of Russia, had long coveted Sweden as a wonderful addition to what she called her "Great Northern Alliance," aka part of her empire. She already ruled Russia, Crimea, Lithuania, and parts of Poland and Finland, and she was firmly aligned with Denmark (a longtime enemy of Sweden that also ruled Norway). For decades, Russia had developed close connections with (and paid bribes to) large numbers of Swedish aristocrats, military officers, and spies. The empress believed it just a matter of time before she conquered Gustav; she considered him a weakling and an idiot, and gave him the nickname "Falstaff" after Shakespeare's fat, vain, boastful, and cowardly character. Like many, Catherine misjudged Gustav's talents.

Gustav III was named after his predecessors Gustav I, also known as Gustav Vasa (ruled 1523–1560), and Gustav II, or Gustavus Adolphus (ruled 1611–1632). The first Gustav was the "Father of the Nation," a ruthless, ambitious king who declared Sweden an absolute monarchy, made the church and all its holdings part of the state, and established a first-rate army. (For a later use of this name, see Joyce Hansen's chapter, "'All Men Are Created Equal.'") His grandson Gustav II—"the Lion of the North"—was a true warrior king, turning Sweden into a major European power and expanding its boundaries. He also pushed Sweden from an almost medieval society into modern times. (His daughter, Queen Christina, ruled Sweden for twenty-two years after his death.)

A tiny fraction of Gustav III's bloodline could be traced to these two legendary kings. But far from being the ruthless, warmongering regent, Gustav III was more interested in theater, literature, and the arts. He read voraciously; wrote poetry and plays; held masquerades, balls, and jousts; and loved finery of all sorts. He even designed an official national costume for the men of his capital city. The suit, in silk or velvet woven in Sweden, consisted of a short jacket with a cape, breeches, and a broad silk sash tied in a large rosette around the waist. The cut (a theatrical blend of Spanish sixteenth-century and medieval Swedish style) was consistent, but colors varied depending on the occasion, from black and vermilion to pale blue and gold to white with flame-red trim. This national costume was thought wonderful by Gustav's supporters and awful by his enemies, but men in Stockholm obliged and wore it daily. The Stockholm ladies had a version of national costume to wear at court, but otherwise insisted on the current fashion from France and England.

Gustav III's love of art, culture, and intellect had a larger impact than frivolity and fashion. He admired modern Enlightenment ideas and adopted some into his leadership. (He was pen pals with Voltaire.) He studied the English parliamentary system and considered it a potential model for Sweden. He established the Swedish Academy to further Swedish literature and language; it is the institution that awards the Nobel Prize in Literature today. Girls as well as boys could receive educations, in contrast to most places in the world at that time. The free press flourished. He started the Royal Dramatic Theater and the Royal Opera, both still producing world-class theater in Stockholm. He brought to his isolated capital a refinement inspired by France—a country (and royal family) to which Gustav had strong ties.

But Gustav's love for Sweden trumped all other passions. Losing honor, territory, or sovereignty was wholly unacceptable, and he would do anything to defend his nation, including actually taking on the role of warrior king.

Prelude to the Riksdag: Stockholm and Swedish Finland, May 1788
Russia had mobilized 200,000 troops in the Baltic against Swedish territory (what is now Finland). Gustav told his advisory council, the Senate, that Sweden must take immediate action. The Senate agreed. Even though existing law required him to get final approval from the Riksdag before going to war, Gustav chose not to. Instead, on Midsummer's Day, 1788, Gustav and his fleet set sail.

The war began in earnest in July, and Gustav's timing was impeccable: Russia's military efforts were concentrated in Turkey against the Ottoman Empire, leaving the north (especially the capital of Saint Petersburg) nearly defenseless. Gustav's ground troops were superior and in position to conquer. Empress Catherine prepared to flee to Moscow, commandeering a thousand horses for transport, but changed her mind and held strong. The sea battles were fierce, and losses for Sweden mounted. The king's brother Duke Karl, admiral of the fleet, botched (perhaps deliberately) a crucial battle. Then, at the end of the month, Finnish regiments revolted and asked to be dismissed from the fighting. A group of thirty-five Swedish officers, aligned with the aristocracy, mutinied against Gustav and attempted to broker peace with Catherine without the king's knowledge. They were joined by even more of the military (known as the Confederation of Anjala), sabotaging any chance of success.

To add to the chaos, Denmark (at the suggestion of Empress Catherine) invaded Sweden. The situation looked dire for Gustav. One imagines his cousin Catherine grinning with delight in Saint Petersburg and his brother Karl trying on the crowns and ermine capes back in Stockholm. But the Danish invasion was exactly the event Gustav needed: it woke Sweden to the dangers all around and gave Gustav an opportunity to play the hero at home. He returned to Sweden, rallied the commoners, and stopped the Danish invasion.

The nobility did little to help, and the citizens took note of their lack of patriotism. The mutinous military officers of Anjala were captured and imprisoned, reviled nationwide as traitors.

The war went on winter break—normal procedure then—and Gustav claimed that victory against Russia was within reach. To win, he needed parliamentary approval for money, ships, and soldiers. He called the Riksdag for January. The previous session (1786) had been a disaster for the king: his legislation voted down, his character attacked, his enemies close to crushing him. This time Gustav intended to get what he wanted and believed the only possible way was to further consolidate his power.

The Meeting of the Riksdag: Stockholm, January–April 1789

The opening of the Riksdag took place on January 26. Ceremonies and preliminaries took up the first days. Each estate was asked to name representatives who would meet with the king in secret to discuss his proposals before bringing them to the entire assembly. Gustav hosted lavishly in the interest of pushing through his agenda, setting up clubs with free liquor, food, and tobacco for all four estates. Two locales were set up for the nobles; not only was their number larger than the other three estates combined, but they also needed the most greasing: of the 950 members (including the king's brother Duke Karl), 700 were declared Patriots, enemies of the king. They preferred the hospitality of Patriot leader Baron De Geer, the wealthiest noble in the realm.

Over two weeks passed. The commoners of the three lower estates obeyed the king, but the Patriot nobility refused to name representatives, insulted Gustav's appointees, and argued violently with his supporters. The clergy hid. The burghers and peasants accused the nobles of cowardice and treachery, making up insulting songs describing them as traitors and paid spies of Russia. Anti-aristocratic pamphlets littered the streets. The citizens of Stockholm gathered to support their king, ready to attack his enemies. Troops were mustered to maintain order.

The work of the nation had ground to a halt, so on February 17, Gustav called the entire assembly to the royal palace. From the solid silver throne of Queen Christina, dressed in purple and ermine robes, and with the crown of Gustavus Adolphus placed firmly on his head, King Gustav III told the First Estate that they were disobedient, unruly, disloyal, and rude, then kicked them out of the palace and told them to go back to their meeting hall and do their jobs. This public humiliation of the aristocracy was a first. The three common estates loved it, as did the cheering crowds gathered around the palace. The outraged nobles retreated to their stately building on Riddarholmen—Knights' Island—where their anger reached a fever pitch. Swords were drawn, insults hurled, plots hatched. Outside on the street, crowds jeered. The king called in his special forces to maintain the peace and keep the nobility under control.

That same afternoon, the three lower estates sent their representatives to meet with the king in the Velvet Chamber of the palace. It was here that Gustav unveiled the Act of Unity and Security—a benign name for such explosive legislation. The act gave the king total executive and legislative power. He alone could declare war, create alliances, and negotiate peace. He alone would appoint and dismiss government functionaries. He could call a meeting of the Riksdag if and when he wanted, and it would only consider matters the king brought to the table. He could decide the number of members in the 500-year-old Senate and decided it was zero. The act substituted the existing constitution with a monarchy very close to absolute despotism but for one important exception: money. The power of the purse was still reserved for the estates.

Gustav knew the Act of Unity and Security would inspire opposition or possibly outright revolt, even with his loyal commoners. So he added three extraordinary paragraphs to the act: male commoners would now be eligible for nearly all offices and dignities of the state; every Swede, even women (with restrictions), would have the ability to purchase land owned by the state and aristocracy; and the nobility would no longer be exempt from taxes and other public burdens. These rights and privileges broke down the long-standing barriers of class. They were the stuff of revolution elsewhere.

Even with these unheard-of offerings, the representatives of the three common estates were utterly shocked by the king's proposal, unsure if they could get enough votes in favor of the act. It was clear to all that the First Estate would rise up in complete rebellion. So Gustav took action again. On February 18, he had twenty-one of his most ferocious and vocal opponents in the nobility arrested and jailed. The next day, the entire Riksdag was again called to order. The king, serene and confident, introduced the Act of Unity and Security and called for a vote. The competing shouts of yes and no required him to call for a vote three times. The results were still inconclusive. The nobles demanded a recess for discussion. The king declared this unnecessary. According to existing law, if three of the four estates adopted legislation, no further discussion was required, and the clergy, burghers, and peasants had voted yes. (This maneuver caused extra pain to the nobles, since it was a law they devised in 1786 to control the king.)

Gustav's power play was effective. Two days later, the three lower estates signed and sealed the Act of Unity and Security in the king's presence without waiting for the First Estate. There was no resistance, no attempt to rescue the imprisoned. The nobility was scared into submission. Duke Karl suddenly declared support for his brother and was made military governor of Stockholm. (Gustav understood the notion of keeping your enemies close.) The common estates and the citizens of Stockholm (men and women) saw their beloved king as a triumphant and benevolent father. Only the "Fifth Estate"—the aristocratic women—rebelled.

Unlike their French counterparts—aristocratic women who supported reform—Swedish women of position and power worked furiously *against* any changes to the status quo rather than for them. Their own standing lay in being part of the nobility; therefore weakening the First Estate weakened their position. They plotted treason with their husbands and lovers. They did not attend court or socialize in any way with the king, something deeply hurtful to him. They gossiped maliciously, spreading rumors of Gustav's depravity and excess that were taken up by the press.

Gustav became more and more isolated, with few friends and allies, but the Fifth Estate failed to stop his forward momentum. In April 1789, the Act of Unity and Security was "approved" by the nobility in a fiercely divided voice vote that the king simply declared in his favor.

The Aftermath: Sweden, 1789 and Beyond

Sweden won the war against Russia, keeping Gustav's cousin Catherine out, though victory came at a staggering financial and human cost. But it was the reforms included in the Act of Unity and Security that had the most dramatic and lasting impact. Four months before the French Revolution broke out in Paris, it was the king himself who began a revolution that pushed Sweden toward class equality.

Why did Gustav, fervent defender of the monarchy, take this radical step? Historians offer several theories. One is that it was a bribe, luring the three lower estates into granting him near despotic power—but power necessary to escape Russian domination. Another theory is more personal: Gustav was deeply hurt and angry at the nobles he believed had betrayed him; the commoners who loved and protected him deserved respect and reward. A third theory rests with Gustav's foresight and political acumen: he saw where the world was heading and thought gradual reform would defuse the ticking time bomb of violent revolution.

Whatever Gustav III's reasons, his 1789 Act of Unity and Security cracked open the door to new, modern structures in society, and the Swedish people took their first steps toward political and economic progress without bloodshed or violence—at least on a large scale. In 1792 King Gustav III was assassinated at a masquerade ball held in the Royal Opera House. The conspiracy involved over two hundred Patriots from the aristocracy, including his brother Duke Karl (who eventually wore the crown). In the end, Gustav III gave his life to the revolution. He lived and died the most contradictory of kings.

PI, VEGA, AND THE BATTLE AT BELGRADE

AMY ALZNAUER

THE NUMBER PI was there from the beginning. A primal secret hidden at the heart of a primal shape. For before the rectangle or triangle had occurred to anyone, the circle, impossible to miss, burned in the orb of the sun, in the round pupil of the eye.

The circle was there on September 28, 1789, when Jurij Vega looked up at the sky after six straight days of rain and saw the sun emerging over the battlefield at Belgrade. It was there in the memory of his new wife he'd left behind in Vienna, in that chain of polished pearls ringing her pale neck, draped in the piled-up curls of her hair. It was there in the iron cannonballs stacked about him, waiting for him to compute the ideal angle for their launch at the Ottomans.

The number pi was also on Vega's mind as he looked about at those stacks of iron balls and remembered the pearls. Only a month before, his brilliant paper on the digits of pi had been read aloud in his absence at the great Saint Petersburg Academy. He wasn't there in Russia, or in Vienna with his wife or at his post as mathematics professor at the artillery school, because he'd signed up of his own accord for war. Trying to convince authorities that a man of his station should march off with the troops, Vega had eagerly written that he believed his mathematics could benefit the battlefield.

But the number pi was on his mind only because of the centuries of thinkers who preceded him. Five years earlier in 1784, the German philosopher Immanuel Kant had penned his rallying cry, "Dare to know!" which soon became a motto for the age. But if people hadn't always, in some real sense, dared to know, pi might have remained forever hidden within the circle. We can practically see those ancient humans, soon after the dawn of history, with their makeshift compasses, their stakes and lengths of rope, drawing circle after circle in the sand.

It wasn't long before they noticed something astounding. The length of rope that stretched exactly across the middle of a circle — *any* circle, no matter how large or small — also fit about three times around its perimeter. In other words, the circumference of any circle was about three times its diameter. It was always the same. How shocking to uncover this numerical secret within the ever-present, everyday circle. It was enough to make you think mathematics lay at the heart of everything. But here was the maddening fact. It never came out at exactly three. There was always a tiny bit of circle left over, a tiny bit of rope left to measure out.

It wasn't until the mid-1700s, right before Vega's birth, that this strange number, slightly larger than three, came to be known as "pi," the first letter in the Greek word for "periphery." Trying to pin down the digits of pi was like the search for the Holy Grail, one of the great quests of humanity. If you looked through history from the vantage of pi, it might even seem that pi itself was an active force, wheeling through time, dipping down now and then to fire up the mind of a new mathematical genius.

So here, in the early fall of 1789, on the battlefield at Belgrade, at the confluence of the Sava and Danube Rivers, pi had alighted again, in the mind of a newly married Slovenian professor of mathematics turned warrior.

In the days of rain preceding the sun's reemergence, thirty-three thousand troops, a quarter of the Austrian army, writhed with illness in their tents. Jurij Vega waited for battle, watching the Sava River rise and Belgrade smoke through the fog.

Perhaps he wondered why he'd chosen, argued even, to come here and face his potential death. But he'd always lived like that, wrenching his life away from tradition. When he was only six years old, his father had died, leaving open the possibility that his future life wouldn't be determined by his past. As he grew older, his family pressured him to stay and tend the farm. But he wanted, needed, an education, so he headed off for Ljubljana and studied with the Jesuits and later at the Lyceum. Soon he proved to be a brilliant calculator and gravitated to mathematics.

Breaking even more definitively with his past, at twenty-five years old he changed his name. Born Veha, which literally meant "unreliable man," he reimagined himself as Vega. Biographers say he simply chose the Germanic version of his name, but the overlap with Vega—the fifth brightest star in the sky, already common in books of astronomy—would not have been lost on him. So, as if to proclaim himself a *lumière*, one of the new enlightened intellectuals fighting against tyranny and tradition for freedom of thought, he went from *unreliable one* to *bright star*.

But why risk snuffing out this light at the hands of the armies of the Ottoman Empire? Sitting there, listening to men groan through the battering rain, Vega, like all other soldiers facing battle, had to shore himself up. Maybe he thought of Archimedes. Often named the greatest mathematician who ever lived, Archimedes had a powerful influence on the mathematics of Vega's time and was, like Vega, both a pure mathematician and an engineer. After his death, Vega himself would come to be known as the Archimedes of Slovenia.

Almost exactly two thousand years before this moment in Belgrade, Archimedes stood on a different battlefield. For years, Archimedes had leveraged mathematics to help the Greeks hold off the Romans at Syracuse. His great war machines launched, as Plutarch would later put it, "immense masses of stone that came down with incredible noise and violence." Archimedes designed machines and calculated accurate trajectories for these missiles, which "knocked down those upon whom they fell in heaps." But the Romans had finally broken through and taken the city. Deeply absorbed with circles he'd drawn in the sand, Archimedes didn't notice. Even when a soldier approached, brandishing his sword, Archimedes only glanced up, his mind lost in geometry, and said, "Do not disturb my circles." The soldier ran him through, leaving him to die amid his sketches.

Peering back through the centuries, from his present battlefield to that ancient one, Vega must have seen Archimedes as a mathematical saint of sorts, a martyr even. Archimedes brought mathematics to bear powerfully against his enemy. And yet he never became merely a warrior. Even on the battlefield, he didn't give in to fear or rage but kept his mind fixed on circles. Mathematics was both a practical tool for changing the world and the reason a better world was worth fighting and even dying for. In such a world, the power and beauty of mathematics could be freely pursued.

And what were those last circles, Vega might have wondered, that Archimedes drew in the sand? Were they his famous sphere and cylinder, which would later be placed on his tomb? Or was Archimedes again thinking through his method for approximating pi?

We can picture Vega, trying to fend off dread or boredom, re-creating these diagrams on the floor of his tent. With the tip of a saber or spade, he draws a circle, as well as possible in the only dry patch of dirt around, and then, following Archimedes's method, plots out six equally spaced points around its outer edge. And finally, with six quick strokes of the spade, a regular hexagon emerges, fitting perfectly inside the circle.

And perhaps he then constructs a regular hexagon around the outside of the circle, again as Archimedes did, until the circle appears to thread between two gears: the inscribed and circumscribed hexagons. Now it is simple: ignore the rain, shut out the moaning, and just calculate the perimeter of the two six-sided polygons, divide each by the diameter, and he has pinned pi between a lower and upper bound.

He can do it again, fend off the growing weight of the sky, this time using polygons with more sides, an octagon, a decagon. The more sides he uses, the more narrowly the circle threads the gears, and the closer the approximation gets. He moves in on pi, closer and closer, as close as he wants actually. The only barrier is the monumental task of calculation. Without recourse to trigonometry or even decimals, Archimedes only managed to wedge pi between two fractions that would yield an approximation of 3.14. But his ingenious method dominated attempts to approximate pi all the way up to the scientific revolution, just a century before Vega.

Vega's mind might have drifted to his own work on pi. As in Archimedes's time, calculation was still formidable. It took a mind like Vega's, able to hold many digits at once, to even attempt the daunting task. He'd cut his calculating teeth on tables of logarithms, accurate to ten decimal places, which filled pages of his unfolding four-volume treatise on mathematics. Confident in the precision of his work, Vega offered a gold ducat to anyone who could find a mistake.

Those were exuberant times back in Vienna. But now, sheltering in his tent at night with nothing to do but wait, Vega must have found Vienna a distant memory. And yet, he was here to fight for Vienna, for Austria. He was a Masonic brother, after all, part of a movement of intellectuals committed to preserving freedom of thought and access to the arts. Under the rule of Joseph II, Austrians believed they had found the key to an enlightened society. How else, they thought, except by the rule of a benevolent king, could you maintain these values? But in just a few years, they would turn and fight equally hard against the French revolutionaries, who also threatened the status quo with their seemingly mad, violent revolt.

Even more likely, though, Vega thought about none of this, but instead tried to steady his mind as Archimedes once had, by focusing on circles. Forget the drone of waiting, he might have told himself. Forget the hum of rain-hammered troops, of drums. Focus.

Unlike Archimedes, Vega did not use polygons to edge in on pi. Now, with the advent of calculus behind him—the work of Sir Isaac Newton and Gottfried Leibniz and Leonhard Euler, all of whom saw their thought growing directly out of Archimedes's—Vega could represent pi instead as an infinite sum, like this one:

$$\pi = 4 \cdot (1 - \tfrac{1}{3} + \tfrac{1}{5} - \tfrac{1}{7} + \tfrac{1}{9} - \ldots)$$

Maybe he scratched it out in the dirt next to the circles. Just as you could increase the number of sides of a polygon to improve the approximation, you could get as close as you wished to pi by summing enough terms. But again, the problem was calculation. It would start out easily enough: $1 - \tfrac{1}{3}$. No problem. Then add $\tfrac{1}{5}$. Fine. But eventually it would take two thousand terms of the infinite series above, computing fractions like $\tfrac{1}{2971}$, to get even three decimal places of accuracy.

So, Vega borrowed a clever formula from Euler. It was similar to the one scratched in the dirt but closed in on pi much more quickly.

After only fifteen steps, this new formula would give pi to twenty-one decimal places. And now he improved on Euler's method, combining positive and negative terms to "telescope" the series, making it collapse upon pi even more rapidly. But still the work was painstaking. Vega had to patiently sweat every one of those 140 digits he finally wrote out in the Saint Petersburg paper.

But did this long labor of his mind really matter? It must have been a hard question during those endless nights of rain. How could his belief in this work not have wavered? After all, if you took a circle with diameter equal to the distance from the earth all the way to the sun and back again, you could compute its colossal circumference to within one millimeter of accuracy with only fifteen digits of pi. There was no practical need, no applied use, for 140 digits, no matter how brilliant and laborious their discovery.

In Vega's time, in the wake of the scientific revolution, people were turning their eyes outward, looking for applications. In the mid-1700s, Denis Diderot had written, "The reign of mathematics is over." And by this he meant the reign of pure mathematics. "Tastes have changed." Later in 1781, just eight years before this battle at Belgrade, the great Joseph-Louis Lagrange wrote about his own growing sense of mathematical malaise. After calculus had taken the world by storm, Lagrange felt that "perfection of details" seemed to be the only thing that remained to be done. Applied fields like physics and chemistry, he said, now offered riches that were "more brilliant and easier to exploit."

But it hadn't always been that way. Back in ancient Greece, the reverse was true. Plutarch apologized profusely for Archimedes's war machines, writing them off as matters of no importance, "mere amusements in geometry." He claimed that Archimedes himself repudiated "as sordid and ignoble the whole trade of engineering." But Archimedes spoke quite differently, gleefully even. "Give me a place to stand on," he cried, "and I will move the earth!" And then he designed a great lever to lift Roman ships out of the sea and then dash them against the rocks. Yet Archimedes was equally a pure mathematician, whose brilliant thinking would loom large through the centuries, all the way to Vega's time.

So even in this, Vega would have found a brother in Archimedes. Yes, Vega had been a navigational engineer on the Mura, Drava, and Sava Rivers. He'd studied the trajectories of heavy mortars. But he was also writing a four-volume series on both pure and applied mathematics. Vega wouldn't have cared about some line drawn in the sand between theory and practice. It was all of a piece. Even mathematicians today write about Vega's wonderful ability to combine "theoretical concerns with practical applications." And unlike Lagrange, Vega relished perfecting the details.

A recent commentator claimed that Vega calculated 140 digits of pi merely to establish his brilliance as a calculator. But this misses the point. Vega was like Archimedes and like his brothers at the Masonic Lodge—a thinker, an intellectual, an artist. To these kinds of people, the details matter. One paint stroke, one note could make or ruin the composition. Vega calculated the minute details of pi because in a free society you could do things like that—write a concerto, paint a masterpiece, chart out the secret of the circle.

Maybe the storm cleared during the night, not the next morning. Maybe Vega looked up and saw not the circle of the sun but the constellation Lyra, its brightest blue-white star, Vega, seeming to declare his purpose in the sky. Yes, the details mattered. There he was, a single man, standing under a single star, with the chance to fight for a better world, a world in which people were free to contemplate pi. And there he was, a single man, who knew better than most how to move the world with the details of his calculations.

Soon he would head out on the battlefield with an armful of

branches. He would run from cannon barrel to cannon barrel, propping each up to adjust the angle of elevation. Then he'd stop, maybe scratch out another calculation in the dirt, and perfectly wedge another branch under a heavy mortar until its missiles would knock down those upon whom they fell in heaps.

The siege would continue, intensifying over the next week. On October 7, 1789, over a seventeen-hour period, 187,000 missiles would rain down with precision on Belgrade, bringing about the Ottoman surrender the next day. And all the while Vega would work, in the midst of battle, without fear or rage. The digits of pi would fly in the background of his thoughts like a banner, proclaiming, "The details matter! Dare to know!"

Vega's record of 140 digits of pi would stand for fifty years, but eventually it would be shown that he was correct only up to 126 digits. And eventually 126 digits would seem like nothing. Soon after Vega's time, pi would be shown to be irrational, meaning its digits go on forever, never repeating a finite pattern. On November 11, 2016, after 105 days of computer time, the Swiss particle physicist Peter Trueb announced over 22.4 trillion digits of pi. In his announcement, Trueb failed to mention anything about the pain or time this calculation cost him, if it cost him anything at all.

The casualties at Belgrade in 1789 were counted by the hundreds. In World War II, the Sajmište concentration camp at Belgrade would annihilate over twenty-three thousand people. But even this would be dwarfed by the millions lost in the two world wars. In 1789 the entire world population was still in the millions. Now we are nearing a dizzying total of eight billion.

When digits come cheap and lives are tallied by the billion, it is easy to forget that we are no different from Vega or even from the now-distant Archimedes. Each one of us is a single human being, standing under the circle of the sun, under a bright star at night, who has a chance to make a difference, to fight for a better, more enlightened world, to believe in the details of our life and work, which together make up our entire life. For how we spend each minute adds up to how we spend our days. And that, of course, day by day, digit by digit, eventually becomes how we spend our lives.

A B O M

THE French had shown themselves the ablest architects of ruin that had hitherto existed in the world. In that very short space of time they had completely pulled down to the ground their monarchy, their church, their nobility, their law, their revenue, their army, their navy, their commerce, their arts, and their manufactures.

[The French revolutionaries] made and recorded a sort of institute and digest of anarchy, called the rights of man, in such a pedantic abuse of elementary principles as would have disgraced boys at school; but this declaration of rights was worse than trifling and pedantic in them; as by their name and authority they systematically destroyed every hold of authority by opinion, religious or civil, on the minds of the people. By this mad declaration they subverted the state; and brought on such calamities as no country, without a long war, has ever been known to suffer, and which may in the end produce such a war, and, perhaps, many such.

— *EDMUND BURKE*, Reflections on the Revolution in France, *1790. In a speech in the House of Commons, Burke condemned the French Revolution, warning others about the danger of an "irrational, unprincipled, proscribing, confiscating, plundering, ferocious, bloody, and tyrannical democracy." He believed that change should occur gradually.*

NATION

T HE *rights of man* have been discussed, till we are somewhat wearied with the discussion. To these have been opposed, as the next stage in the progress of illumination, and with more presumption than prudence, *the rights of women*. It follows, according to the natural progression of human things, that the next influx of that irradiation, which our enlightenment is pouring in upon us, will illuminate the world with grave descants on the *rights of youth—the rights of children—the rights of babies!*

> —*HANNAH MORE*, Strictures of the Modern System of Female Education, *1799. Despite urging female education and public roles for women, the English poet and playwright was politically conservative and decidedly anti-feminist. Here, More is writing satirically. Interestingly, More named her two cats "Passive Obedience" and "Non-Resistance."*

THE QUEEN'S CHEMISE

—◆—

ÉLISABETH VIGÉE LE BRUN, PORTRAITIST OF MARIE ANTOINETTE

SUSAN CAMPBELL BARTOLETTI

IN 1761 six-year-old Marie-Louise-Élisabeth Vigée was already an artist. With charcoal and chalk pastels, Élisabeth drew faces and landscapes on everything. She decorated the margins of her school notebooks and those of her friends and classmates, and drew on the dormitory walls of her French convent boarding school.

The next year Élisabeth, now seven, bent over a wooden table. In a circle of yellow lamplight, she sketched a man with a beard and presented the drawing to her father, Louis Vigée. A successful but minor portrait artist, Vigée recognized promise and talent when he saw it. Clutching his young daughter's artwork, he proclaimed, "You will be a painter, child, if ever there was one."

And Élisabeth would be, although her father wouldn't live to enjoy her success. Five years later, Louis Vigée swallowed a fishbone that became lodged in his throat. The surgeon was called, but the surgery was unsuccessful and infection set in. Vigée died an agonizing death two months later.

In pre-revolutionary France, as in other Western countries, women had no political rights. They could not vote. Their rights to property, financial independence, education, work, and other opportunities were restricted.

Vigée's death left the family penniless. With few options, Élisabeth's widowed mother soon married again. Twelve-year-old Élisabeth detested her stepfather, a wealthy but miserly jeweler who insisted on wearing her father's clothing. In her memoir, *Souvenirs*, Élisabeth wrote that her stepfather was too stingy to have the ill-fitting clothes altered.

Mourning her father, Élisabeth threw herself into her work and found comfort in her art. By sixteen, Élisabeth was acquiring important clients—nobles and aristocrats and wealthy men and women—who commissioned her to paint their portraits and portraits of their children. The money wasn't hers to keep. She was expected to contribute to household expenses and to pay for her younger brother's education. Her stepfather pocketed her earnings, as was his right.

As Élisabeth developed her skill, she learned how to give her clients what they wanted. Using a bright palette, she would capture their personality in an unguarded, fresh-faced, and flattering way. Her portraits exuded charm and sensitivity, showing a deep respect for her subjects—and always enhanced their looks.

During this time, many Enlightenment philosophers were questioning traditional ideas about politics and society. Does a king have a divine right to rule? Does a king's power come from God or from the people? Shouldn't citizens have the right to remove a king from power? Couldn't man infinitely perfect himself and others through education and reason? Wasn't it important for men to reason for themselves? Shouldn't men have equality under the law? Weren't men imbued with natural rights—the rights of liberty and equality— simply because they were men? Why should men be relegated to one social class? Shouldn't class be based upon merit—what a man accomplishes—and not birth?

Enlightenment artists and writers—again, *men*, for the cries of *liberté* and *égalité* were for and about the *fraternité*, or brotherhood, in pre-revolutionary France—were also questioning the role of the artist and the purpose of art. Shouldn't art serve a purpose? Shouldn't art consider the public? Shouldn't art be moral? Didn't art have an obligation to uplift and teach people right from wrong? The aim of art, wrote the French philosopher Denis Diderot, was "to make virtue attractive, vice odious, ridicule forceful; that is the aim of every honest man who takes up the pen, the brush, or the chisel."

Most Enlightenment thinkers—again, men—took a traditional position on "the woman question." They argued that a woman's place was in the private sphere and that women didn't need an equal education to prepare them for life.

As a female artist, Élisabeth was allowed to take drawing lessons but wasn't permitted to study the nude human figure, an essential part of a serious artist's education. This restriction deprived her from training at the prestigious Académie Royale de Peinture et de Sculpture, where such study took place. Even private lessons were reserved for male artists only.

It might seem that Élisabeth would have longed for change. But as other artists swung left politically and French women began to demand more rights, Élisabeth remained conservative in her politics and in her art. She supported the monarchy, as her father had. She didn't paint to teach or to convey messages or the principles of Enlightenment ideology in her work. She painted to please her well-to-do clients and to make money. For her, art was as much a commodity as it was her gift.

And make money she did. By the time twenty-year-old Élisabeth married the art dealer Jean-Baptiste-Pierre Le Brun, she had painted well over one hundred portraits. Other female artists put away their brushes and paints when they married and turned their lives to taking care of their home and family, as was expected of women. But not Élisabeth. She continued to paint.

After marriage, Élisabeth's reputation as a portraitist continued to grow, and she won increasingly important commissions. Two years later, in 1778, word of her talent reached the inner circle at Versailles. Queen Marie Antoinette's mother, the empress Maria Theresa of Austria, wanted a portrait of her daughter.

To oblige her mother, Marie Antoinette summoned Élisabeth Vigée Le Brun to the palace at Versailles.

"All the Graces—All the Nobility"

Élisabeth traveled by carriage through the French countryside to reach the palace of Versailles that stood twelve miles outside Paris. She was ushered through the guard room to the queen's sumptuous private apartment.

There stood Marie Antoinette, queen of France, the most important woman in France and possibly the world, wearing a voluminous court dress of white satin, as wide as she was tall, with expensive silk ribbons and gold tassels and a feathery headdress. The queen's unpowdered ash-brown hair was piled high in an elaborate, towering pouf, spilling down her neck.

Élisabeth Vigée Le Brun, *Marie Antoinette en robe à paniers
(Marie Antoinette in Court Dress)*, 1778, oil on canvas.

Later Élisabeth admitted how she trembled in Marie Antoinette's presence. "To anyone who has not seen the queen," wrote Élisabeth, "it is difficult to get an idea of all the graces and all the nobility combined in her person." But, she added, "Her Majesty spoke to me so graciously that my fear soon dissipated."

Élisabeth set to work, trying especially hard to please the queen and to show off her talent. This opportunity was the commission of a lifetime. If successful, her work would bring her the greatest amount of money she had ever earned for one painting—and the possibility of more opportunities. The money wouldn't be hers to keep; her husband had the right to claim her earnings, which he did.

Élisabeth made several quick studies. Looking past the queen's imposing figure, Élisabeth found a long and oval face, merry and kind almost-blue eyes more narrow than wide, a slender nose, and a small mouth with thick lips.

As she prepared her palette, she was struck by the queen's complexion. "I never have seen one so brilliant, and brilliant is the word, for her skin was so transparent that it bore no umber in the painting," wrote Élisabeth. "Neither could I render the real effect of it as I wished. I had no colors to paint such freshness, such delicate tints, which were hers alone, and which I had never seen in any other woman."

The resulting painting, *Marie Antoinette en robe à paniers* (*Marie Antoinette in Court Dress*), is a full-length, formal rendering of the queen, a portrait that reveals little about the woman we've come to know as Marie Antoinette. Nor are any of the character traits that Élisabeth notes in her *Souvenirs*—the queen's merry and kind eyes, her wit and charm, for example—revealed. Instead, the pictorial space is crowded with symbols and objects that tell their own dramatic story about the queen.

Marie Antoinette stands front and center, a formidable triangle framed in a doorway next to a table draped with expensive velvet cloth woven from silk. On top of a blue velvet pillow embroidered with fleurs-de-lis sits a gold crown studded with diamonds, gemstones, and pearls. A vase holds pink roses, the queen's favorite flower and an homage to her Austrian heritage; behind the vase a partial painting can be seen, likely an allegory. Above on the gilded mantel sits a bust of the young king himself, Louis XVI, who watches over his queen.

There's no doubt that this rendering shows off Élisabeth's virtuosity. The painting is a tour-de-force, filled with triangles, rectangles, circles, sumptuous textures, light and shadow, values and hues, and movement. She invites the viewer's eye to move past the bust of Louis XVI to the cascades of blue drapery, to the room beyond, around the curved column and the rose chair trimmed with gold that holds the train of the court dress, and then across the embroidered carpet, circling back to the young queen herself, who seems to float, as radiant as a shimmering golden orb, tethered by one pointy ivory-slippered foot. The light comes from the left, illuminating her skin, and wraps around her.

Marie Antoinette doesn't meet the viewer's eye but gazes offstage in a way that invokes a feeling of emotional and psychic distance in the viewer. This is a queen who has power and wealth, but lacks freedom. This is a queen who enjoys the privileges of the court, but detests its formality and hierarchy. This is a queen who longs to escape the court's restrictions and conventions and restraints, all so present in this painting.

Nonetheless, the empress Maria Theresa was delighted with the rendering. "Your large portrait pleases me!" she wrote her daughter. Élisabeth would return to Versailles to paint Marie Antoinette and her family more than thirty times over the next ten years, more than any other artist.

A "Remarkably Stupid" Queen

In 1769 Marie Antoinette was a frivolous fourteen-year-old arch-duchess named Maria Antonia Josepha Johanna who left Austria to marry fifteen-year-old Louis XVI, her second cousin. On a neutral island in the middle of the Rhine River, Maria Antonia relinquished her Austrian identity—her clothing, her jewelry, and even her little pug, Mops, who was considered an Austrian citizen. She became French and took the name Marie Antoinette. (After much negotiation, Marie Antoinette and her dog were reunited.)

Marie Antoinette soon developed a reputation for spending France's money—money the country, greatly in debt, did not have. Her lavish dresses, her elaborate hairstyles, and her shoes became trending news in gossip circles and fashion magazines that were published as often as every ten days. What Marie Antoinette wore, Western women clamored to wear.

There's little doubt that the young queen enjoyed her status as a fashion icon and trendsetter. Her style sense was savvy, but she was not savvy when it came to gauging the changing political climate. Or perhaps the queen was able to gauge the climate, but she didn't care or didn't think the rumors and gossip and the French people's need for a scapegoat would touch her. At a time when the average French worker earned two *livres* a day, the queen couldn't empathize with their poverty, couldn't sympathize with their crushing taxes, and couldn't understand the hunger of the commoners—the Third Estate—for *fraternité*, *liberté*, and *égalité*. Marie Antoinette was, as one professor of art history has noted, "a remarkably stupid person."

A staunch believer in absolute royal power and in the divine right of kings, Marie Antoinette likely thought such power and divine right would protect and even save her from the rising tide of populist anger. Through it all, Élisabeth would remain fiercely loyal to the queen.

In 1783 Élisabeth and her husband traveled to Flanders, Belgium. In a gallery, Élisabeth viewed *The Straw Hat*, an oil painting rendered by Peter Paul Rubens in 1625. Feeling inspired, Élisabeth painted herself, also in a three-quarter-length pose.

In her 1783 self-portrait, Élisabeth stands out-of-doors, taking advantage of natural light. She's wearing a simple, rose-colored, loose-style dress and a straw hat with an ostrich feather and a rustic garland of blue, white, and red wildflowers whose colors match the paint on her palette.

The light source comes from the left, casting a partial shadow on her face, but her skin is bright. Her right hand extends forward in a welcoming gesture, and in her left hand, she's holding her palette and paintbrushes as she looks straight on, smiling as she meets the gaze of the viewer. The self-portrait exudes confidence and pride. Here Élisabeth proclaims herself as an artist who is attractive, assertive, and secure in her femininity and identity as she faces the onlooker. In this painting, Élisabeth challenges traditionalists who hold conventional views of womanhood. Here, Élisabeth shows a woman of strength and independence.

Later Élisabeth noted that this painting was instrumental in her election to the Académie Royale de Peinture et de Sculpture, a distinction few female artists achieved, and even fewer women from the Third Estate. In actuality, it was Élisabeth's allegorical painting *La paix qui ramene* (*Peace Bringing Back Abundance*) that won her admission—and Marie Antoinette's intervention, a fact that Élisabeth downplayed in her *Souvenirs*.

Élisabeth Vigée Le Brun, *Autoportrait au chapeau de paille
(Self-Portrait with a Straw Hat)*, 1783, oil on canvas.

At the same time, another female artist, Adélaïde Labille-Guiard, also won admission, and the two women earned the right to display their paintings in the prestigious biennial Salon at the Louvre. Soon vicious accusations circulated that Élisabeth and Adélaïde didn't create their own work and that their paintings were rendered by a male artist. Others accused Élisabeth of having an affair. Some claimed that Élisabeth and Adélaïde were rivals, fueling the mean-spirited and untrue trope that women can't be friends or colleagues, only enemies.

Élisabeth liked her self-portrait well enough to suggest painting Marie Antoinette also wearing a straw hat and a loose-style dress that same year. Marie Antoinette agreed, even wearing Élisabeth's straw hat and ostrich plume. The painting would have great repercussions for the painter and her queen.

In *La reine en gaulle* (*Chemise of the Queen*), Marie Antoinette stands at a table. The queen is all light against a dark background. She's wearing a loose white dress that has full sleeves, a flounced oval neckline, and a sheer golden sash tied in a bow at the waist. Her straw hat is topped with a blue ostrich plume and matching satin ribbon.

The queen's fingers are wrapping a blue satin ribbon around the stem of a pink rose, a symbol of her heritage and also a symbol of love. She is smiling slightly as she gazes sideways, as if she's thinking about someone, and if she is, the someone might be the Swedish military attaché Count Axel von Fersen, whom, it's been speculated, she deeply loved. Again, the queen's face and skin are radiant.

Unlike the earlier portrait, *Marie Antoinette in Court Dress*, *Chemise of the Queen* offers no formal dress or jewelry or objects to signify her status as the queen of France. When the portrait was unveiled at the Salon, its viewers were furious. The *gaulle* was too close in appearance to a muslin undergarment known as a chemise. A chemise was

Élisabeth Vigée Le Brun, *La reine en gaulle*
(Chemise of the Queen), 1783, oil on canvas.

something that women wore next to their skin, underneath their corsets and hoopskirts and gowns.

The dress wasn't a new style. On warm summer days, the queen and her circle of female friends often wore chemises as they walked about the gardens of the Petit Trianon, the queen's private chateau built on the grounds of Versailles.

But to the French people, the queen was posing in an undergarment and smiling about it. A French fashion magazine, *Gallerie des Modes et Costumes Français*, mocked the painting, publishing an engraving of the work with the caption *"Chemise à la reine,"* or "The Queen's Undergarment." Gossip spread quickly. Wicked people, wrote a distraught Élisabeth, said that she had dared to paint the queen in her underwear.

If Marie Antoinette wore a chemise, so would Western women. The chemise quickly took over the fashion world. An aristocrat would later blame the dress—so crucial in defining social identity—for the downfall of French society. "With this revolution in dress came a revolution in good manners," Auguste-François Fauveau de Frénilly wrote in his *Recollections*. After all, if a queen could be seen in her underwear, etiquette was clearly dead.

As the demand for muslin grew, French silk merchants railed against the queen, too. The muslin fabric supported the British cotton industry, for nearly all cotton was imported from India, a British colony. The silk merchants considered it unpatriotic for their queen to wear a British fabric. Her loyalties were already questionable due to her Austrian heritage, and now the fabric confirmed her lack of allegiance to France.

The outrage mounted. Élisabeth quickly turned to damage control. If she didn't already know it, she did now: composition, pose, and costume produce identities. It mattered how a woman presented herself. It didn't matter what Élisabeth or the queen wanted. It mattered what the public wanted.

That same year, Élisabeth rendered a more formal painting and swapped it for the original. In this second painting, the three-quarter-length pose is the same. Marie Antoinette holds a pink rose, as she did before, but she's standing slightly back from the viewer, more distant and elevated than before.

Marie Antoinette looks splendid and regal and yet soft and graceful in the blue satin court dress with its lace and flounces and ribbons. Two strands of pearls loop around her neck. Instead of a common straw hat, she wears an elegant turban-style hat that matches her dress. Her eyes are bright blue and not quite as wide as the earlier version, her hair is powdered and coiffed, and her skin glows.

But the damage was done. The French people weren't going to stand for a queen who challenged their perception of monarchy. They wanted a queen who looked and acted like a queen.

If this painting conveys any message, it might be this: Élisabeth shows us that Marie Antoinette is both feminine and privileged, and yet she also shows us a woman who must negotiate two opposing worlds, a natural world with trees and blue sky and clouds, and an unnatural world with its artifices of human-made rules and conventions.

A World Turned Upside Down

Before his death, Élisabeth's father had made a second prophecy. One night he returned home, moody and depressed, from a dinner where he had met Denis Diderot. When Élisabeth's mother pressed her husband to tell her what had upset him, Louis Vigée said, "All that I have heard tonight, my dear, makes me believe that the world will soon be turned upside down."

Élisabeth Vigée Le Brun, *Marie Antoinette à la rose*
(*Marie Antoinette with a Rose*), 1783, oil on canvas.

In 1787 Élisabeth painted Marie Antoinette and her three children for what would be the final time. At the Petit Trianon, the queen's private hideaway that had cost the French taxpayers two million francs three years earlier, Élisabeth styled the queen's hair, made separate studies of her three children, and then determined the painting's composition.

Like the 1778 painting *Marie Antoinette in Court Dress*, this painting, too, is tour-de-force theater. At the center sits Marie Antoinette, again a triangle, but this time a loving mother surrounded by her children—a composition reminiscent of Raphael's *Madonna*. Élisabeth shows that this woman, now the scapegoat of France, is also a real human being, a mother who has a passionate love for her children and who has suffered a great loss. The queen's infant daughter Sophie had died recently, before her first birthday.

Marie Antoinette wears a formal red velvet dress. Her firstborn daughter, Marie-Thérèse, also wearing a red dress and green sash that circles her waist, leans against her mother in a loving embrace. The queen's second son, Louis-Charles, dressed in a white gown and cap and tiny white slippers, sits in her lap. As any mother would, she holds him tight as he tries to crawl away. Louis Joseph, heir to the throne, stands close by, pulling back a covering and pointing to the now-empty crib.

In this final portrait, the light source is darker, perhaps a winter light. Unlike Raphael's *Madonna*, however, Marie Antoinette is an imposing figure, a matriarch. With a serious gaze, she looks straight at the viewer. Perhaps she knows what the viewer knows, that the hearts of the French people have hardened against her. That Paris is seething. That the Revolution is drawing near and is about to burst out. That her world will soon be turned upside down. That absolute power and divine right cannot save her or prevent the terrible things that will happen to her children.

Élisabeth Vigée Le Brun, *Marie Antoinette, reine de France, et ses enfants
(Marie Antoinette and Her Children)*, 1787, oil on canvas.

Two years later, on October 5, 1789, Parisian mobs invaded Versailles with pikes and pitchforks. The mobs escorted Marie Antoinette and her husband and their children to the Tuileries, the royal palace in Paris, and placed them under house arrest.

Élisabeth understood that her conservative views and close ties with the queen jeopardized her life and that of her nine-year-old daughter, Julie. Already separated from her philandering husband, Élisabeth fled France with Julie. In her pocket, Élisabeth had only twenty francs, although she had earned more than a million; her husband had gambled the rest away.

For the next sixteen years, Élisabeth painted portraits of the rich and famous as she and her daughter traveled throughout Italy, Austria, Czechoslovakia, Germany, Russia, and England. Once she was assured it was safe, Élisabeth returned to Paris, alone, in 1805. By then, Julie was estranged from her mother and married to a man she would later leave.

Until her death in 1842, Élisabeth continued to cultivate a list of celebrity clients—nobility, aristocrats, and other wealthy and notable people—and would remain loyal to the memory of Marie Antoinette. Over her lifetime, Élisabeth rendered over nine hundred works, mostly portraits. Today her work is held in museums, galleries, and private collections around the world. Élisabeth Vigée Le Brun is recognized as an artist who navigated seemingly opposing worlds.

THE CHOICE

PARIS, 1789

MARC ARONSON

PICTURE THIS: you were born enslaved yet are now, tempo-
rarily, free; you are sixteen years old, pregnant, and you must
make the decision that will define your life and your child's. Bound
up in that choice is the meaning of freedom, of liberty, of love, of
revolution—and it is all up to you.

You are in Paris in the spring of 1789. There are rumblings of new
ideas all around you; the streets are filled with performers, speakers,
and protesters. The servants in the home rented for your master, the
American ambassador, all sense that change is in the air. And freedom is available to you in France. There are no slave sales in Paris, no
Africans in chains led off from ships, no posters offering rewards for
capturing escaped slaves.

While French planters make fortunes from the labor of enslaved
people working the sugar islands of the Caribbean, courts in Paris
generally side with any enslaved person brought to France who

claims his or her right to freedom. Freedom is somewhere outside your door—for you, for your unborn child, perhaps for France. You know this because your brother James came here before you, has learned French, and has a good job. He could take you by the hand and walk you to the courtroom doorway through which you would pass to a new life. Other enslaved people have taken that path to freedom—he knows it, you know it; the way is open for you.

Imagine the life you could have here as a new nation is born. But if you stay, you give up your family back in Virginia: you will never see them again. You give up the land you have known since birth, and you give up your lover and the father of your child, perhaps your true love; the most brilliant man you, and most people, have ever met: Thomas Jefferson. He is returning to Virginia, and he wants you and James—who is also enslaved but whom Jefferson paid to have trained as a chef—to return with him.

Return to what? To being owned. A slave is all you can ever be in his Monticello home. Yet perhaps you sense that he really does love you, too. You will have a life—of a kind—together. Impossible as it may seem to twenty-first-century eyes, Sarah (known as Sally) Hemings faced this choice. Her life was already deeply entangled with Jefferson's, as it had been even before she was born.

Jefferson had been married to Martha Wayles, who was weakened by a series of pregnancies and in the summer and fall of 1782 fell fatally ill after giving birth once again. As she faded, Martha called to her bedside her husband, her children, and the enslaved women to whom she was especially close. According to one account, she then told her husband that "she could not die happy, if she thought her four children were ever to have a stepmother. . . . Holding her hand, Mr. Jefferson promised her solemnly that he would never marry again." Sally Hemings was one of those enslaved women by Martha's bedside—Martha, her half-sister.

Sally's grandmother was a woman we cannot trace who was born in Africa and brought to America as a slave. She had a child, Elizabeth, with an English seaman, Captain Hemings, who wanted to purchase their daughter. But Elizabeth was already owned by John Wayles, who refused to sell her. Indeed, John went on to have six children with Elizabeth, including Sally; at the same time, with his white wife Martha Eppes, he fathered Martha Wayles, who would later marry Thomas Jefferson. The one person who was with Martha throughout her entire life, down to that last moment at her bedside, was Elizabeth Hemings—who was both her father's lover and Sally's mother. Martha understood that while the Hemingses were legally her property, they were also her family. After she died, the Hemings family moved to Monticello—to be as closely woven into Jefferson's world as they had been to Martha's. Jefferson could never marry Sally Hemings—her African grandmother made that impossible. But Sally may have understood that the vow he made to Martha left a gap in his life. He needed a companion, a mother to bear and rear his children, a person to share (some of) his days. As one of his closest friends remarked, Sally could become Jefferson's "substitute for a wife." But did Sally Hemings need Thomas Jefferson? Did she really have a choice?

According to Professor Annette Gordon-Reed, the Pulitzer Prize–winning scholar of the Hemings family, all of these layers were there in Sally's mind: the real possibility that she could have a life as a free woman in Paris, the mood of change and excitement in the dawning French Revolution, her enslavement in Virginia, and, most probably for both Jefferson and Hemings, love.

Could Gordon-Reed be right? The chance that Jefferson was manipulating and abusing Hemings is so great, how could it possibly be that they were actually in love? Gordon-Reed carefully examined the whole history of the Hemings family in America, across generations, trying to understand them not through Jefferson's eyes, not as enslaved people or victims, but in terms of how each of them might have seen their world, their own lives. Reading through every possible piece of evidence, and each historian's commentary, Gordon-Reed came to see Sally as a person with her own needs, her own desires, her own feelings. Sally really did have a choice, and we need to understand her decision. At the same time, and again relying on the best current historical scholarship, we need to map out what Sally Hemings may have meant to Thomas Jefferson.

There is something almost too perfect about this moment: 1789. So much seemed to be hanging in the balance with the most glorious future possible for humanity. In 1789, liberty, rights, science, and knowledge were this torch, this blazing light that could uplift all, free all from tyranny, ignorance, and superstition. Jefferson was carried away by that mood. He floated the idea that every nineteen years—a new generation by his calculation—the people of a nation should have the right to entirely break free of the past, cancel debts, and write new rules. The earth, he said, belongs only to the living for them to use. The dead, even the laws written by the dead, must not, zombie-like, control the living. But this magical moment was cursed, for Jefferson could not free himself from his attachment to the most complete form of tyranny, the most rigid form of the past binding the present: the buying, selling, and owning of other human beings, even one whom he may have loved and who was the mother of his children.

Could it be that Jefferson was the kind of manipulator who hides his misuse of others behind high-sounding words: a master wordsmith who uses those closest to him? Was he simply intimidating or sweet-talking Sally into betraying herself to serve his needs? After all, not only was he her owner, but he was forty-four and she a teenager—in every possible way, he had power over her. Sally was known to be "very handsome"—a term used for both men and women at the time—and "mighty near white," perhaps both in complexion and due to the "straight hair" that fell "down her back." Indeed, not surprisingly, she was said to especially resemble Martha Wayles, her half-sister. Was Jefferson, like some monster in a horror movie, forcing a teenager to play the part of his dead wife?

Jefferson believed in his own dreams of liberty. He so hated enslavement that in his original draft of the Declaration of Independence, the longest clause explaining why the new nation needed to break free was his claim that the king had imposed the horror of slavery on the colonies (others removed this clause). And yet he also resisted immediate emancipation, and his wealth rested on the labor of the enslaved people he owned. He argued that Africans were racially inferior and insisted that whites and blacks should not have children together. Yet he treated his own mixed children, and his wife's mixed relations, as special. The Hemings men were free to leave Monticello and look for paid work; the women of the family were never asked to labor in the fields. And we have good reason to believe that Sally clearly understood the choice before her: freedom in Paris, living alone or with her brother, or enslavement at home with Jefferson and her family.

Jefferson was wealthy, a prominent and admired man on two continents, but beyond his résumé, he was extraordinarily charming. He could win over almost anyone, and he spent money buying fabrics and having clothes specially made for Sally. As Gordon-Reed suggests, it is quite possible that Sally would have been flattered by his attention and drawn to his brilliance. After all, throughout her life, from birth on, she had lived in a world of relationships crossing between white and black, owner and enslaved. "No young girl," Gordon-Reed argues, "was better prepared by the complex nature of her family configuration and her life to date to take seriously the professed intentions of a man whom, by any system of logic, she should have seen as an enemy."

Madison Hemings was one of Jefferson and Hemings's children, though not the one she was carrying in Paris (who would be named Tom). According to Madison, while in Paris Sally thought of herself as free. She knew she could walk out the door into a permanently free life. Viewing their relationship as just an older man's cynical seduction of a susceptible teenager misses the complexity of the moment—both the heady atmosphere of revolutionary Paris and the tangled histories of their two families.

Jefferson arrived in Paris in 1784 as the American ambassador. France had helped the United States win its independence, and now American ideas of democracy, liberty, and government were spreading through France. All of humanity seemed to be transforming, opening up. For Jefferson, who had experienced the world turned upside down in America, the feeling of hope, of possibility, was overwhelming. He was like a surfer riding the crest of the most powerful wave—the irresistible surge of human progress. As Thomas Paine, his friend and the author of *Common Sense*, wrote, "From what we now see, nothing of reform on the political world ought to be held improbable. It is an age of revolutions, in which everything may be looked for." Freedom, liberty, and the sense that a new age was dawning were intoxicating to Jefferson. He was drunk on hope and expectation.

Stationed in Paris in 1789, Jefferson was in the middle of the tumult as the French stumbled from financial crisis into governmental reform. He had seen, in his own life, an impossible dream come true, and in Paris he seemed to be living a new version of the 1776 moment. Jefferson held a "school of revolution" with eager French leaders who clustered around George Washington's friend and ally the Marquis de Lafayette. Jefferson commented and consulted on a version of a declaration of rights that Lafayette crafted and the National Assembly adopted as the Declaration of the Rights of Man and of the Citizen—the central statement of their revolution. Jefferson helped to draft the defining documents of two revolutions. The French declaration echoed the American Declaration of Independence and went further. People are "born free and remain free and equal," it announced, and it went on to define freedom as the right "to do everything that injures no one else."

Setting down on paper principles that wiped away thousands of years of royal and aristocratic privilege and that heralded totally new forms of government on both sides of the Atlantic—no wonder Jefferson was light-headed. Yet the grand ideals of the French Declaration of the Rights of Man were as contested as the fine words of the American Declaration of Independence. For example, from 1789 to 1799, as France struggled through varying forms of revolutionary government, it kept changing the rules on overseas slavery. While a small group of idealistic abolitionists wanted to end the practice entirely and briefly succeeded (only to have slavery in the sugar colonies reintroduced by Napoléon), slave owners both white and of mixed background were completely opposed to the idea. The debate over what "born free and equal" meant clashed into the many layers of society on the French sugar islands: Who is free? Whites? Mixed people? Everyone?

As changing and confusing signals came from Paris, the main French sugar colony of Saint-Domingue (now Haiti) erupted into revolt. One of the leaders of the rebellion tied the fight directly to words Jefferson had helped to write. "Have you forgotten," he demanded of his opponents, "that you have formally sworn to the Declaration of Rights . . . which says that men are born free and equal?" As president of the United States, John Adams sent guns to support the uprising. While Jefferson continued to believe in and defend the French Revolution, when he succeeded Adams as president, he was totally opposed to the Haitian rebellion. That does not mean his words were empty, but it does mean that what he could immortalize as a principle he could not always face as a reality. And that was not the only contradiction in Jefferson.

Paris was electrifying to Jefferson. He was a handsome widower with a quick mind. As one observer said of him, Jefferson's conversations were "loose and rambling, and yet he scattered information wherever he went, and some even brilliant sentiments sparkled from him." Now this tall, lively hero of the American Revolution was surrounded by intelligent, beautiful women eager to meet him. Paris was famous—or notorious—for the level of flirtation and erotic intrigue that was considered not merely permissible but even favored as a kind of sport. Benjamin Franklin, for one, reveled in the attentions of French women. Like Alexander Hamilton, Jefferson enjoyed flirting with women and, like Hamilton, may have even engaged in an affair with a married woman: the ravishing Maria Cosway. Their surviving letters show the flow of rising and falling feelings that come from an intensely passionate couple being together and apart. Ever since those letters were found, historians have been like a social network rumor mill trying to determine did they or didn't they—how far did the relationship go?

Jefferson ultimately wrote Cosway an endlessly examined letter about the split between the head and the heart that may have been his way of easing out of the affair. Indeed, the atmosphere of delicious seduction pressed on another divide in Jefferson. In one way, to be seen as a handsome, brilliant wit by the most beautiful, outspoken women of Paris was heaven to him. And yet he thought this whole model of relations between men and women was wrong, destructive, and most dangerous for his own daughters. When he sent for his teenaged daughter Polly to come join him and his elder daughter, Martha (known as Patsy), in Paris, he wanted Polly to be accompanied by an older woman. And though he was a Protestant, the minute Polly arrived he swept her off to join her sister at a convent school to be watched over by Catholic nuns. Paris offered a kind of freedom he could not have at home. And for that very reason, it was an illicit, dangerous place.

No older woman was available to sail with Polly. And that is why Sally was sent—to be the companion protecting a teenage girl. And yet that is precisely what she was—an even more defenseless teenage girl. As an enslaved person, she was completely subject to being abused by men at any stage of the journey. Fortunately, Sally and Polly made the trip without incident, and the young women first landed in London, where they were watched over by Abigail Adams, a family friend of Jefferson's. In time, though, Jefferson and Abigail's husband, future president John Adams, would become bitter political enemies.

When Sally finally arrived safely in Paris, Jefferson faced an initial choice that he had already experienced with her brother James, who had been Jefferson's companion in France since they had arrived in 1784. By French law, any slave owner was required to list the slaves he was bringing into France—his human "property." However, this risked alerting the enslaved people to their right to go to court to sue for freedom. And it would be most embarrassing for Jefferson, who was arriving in Paris as the beacon of the land of liberty. Jefferson chose to call James and Sally his servants instead and advised a fellow slave-owning American in France to do the same. Proof that he was a liar? Yes and no.

Jefferson was certainly lying. But in fact he did pay both James and Sally a weekly salary, and at a rate rather better than his French servants. He paid for James to take French lessons and for his culinary training. Was he buying their silence? Yes, but he was also treating them as what he said they were: salaried staff. And this adds to the Sally mystery. Jefferson's daughters were in school and only came home on Sundays; so what was Sally being paid to do? There were French servants to do housework. At first this was not a question—for soon after Sally landed, Jefferson sent her off to have an expensive set of treatments that would inoculate her against smallpox. Why did he spend the money to get the best doctors for a person he owned? Jefferson believed in science, in medicine, in inoculation. In this case he was willing to pay to put his beliefs into practice. He had requested that Polly's companion be someone who had experienced (or been inoculated against) the disease. He was determined to make sure no carrier of smallpox would be in his household.

What does Jefferson's Paris year of 1789 tell us?

When Jefferson helped to draft his two declarations, the idea that nobles were superior to common people was almost universal, and slavery was legal, accepted, and practiced throughout the world. To call all people equal *was* revolutionary. But Jefferson could not accept the full consequences of his own words.

Jefferson, the extremist ready, in the abstract, to throw out all laws and contracts every nineteen years; Jefferson, the calculating and pragmatic slave owner lying to protect his "property"; Jefferson, the flirtatious man about town; Jefferson, the controlling father; Jefferson, the contributor to two declarations that enshrined human rights; Jefferson, the politician violently opposed to the revolt in Haiti—the second country in the Americas to fight for independence: all of these conflicting sides of his personality were on display in Paris. The truth is in his contradictions: head and heart each holding equal claims—not one side hiding another. And one more truth: Jefferson craved being admired, being loved. He admitted to his grandchildren, "It is charming to be loved by everybody." In his "Head and Heart" letter to Maria Cosway, "Head" had said that

"Heart" complained that to be separated from loved ones "is worse than death, inasmuch as this ends our sufferings, whereas that only begins them: and that the separation would in this instance be the more severe as you would probably never see them again." He was speaking of the Cosways, but the same applied to the Hemings family.

Jefferson could have offered to leave James and Sally in Paris with a bit of money—out of sight, the pregnancy and mixed-race relationship an ocean away from his critics in America who were sure to find out about it. But he didn't. He asked James and Sally to return with him. He didn't just want to own them; he wanted them to love him. And that was not just a general need for affection. As one of his Hemings descendants recalled, "Jefferson loved her dearly."

What of Sally? What does her stay in Paris tell us?

Sally may well have explored the city with her brother—they had time and money; he spoke the language and had local connections. They had every right to walk out into Paris just as the city was the very center of a nation finding a way toward a new kind of law, of freedom; just as their owner helped to write those laws.

Sally faced that divide, that absolute choice—France or America—with a great deal of knowledge. According to Madison Hemings, Sally had begun to learn French and she understood that "in France she was free, while if she returned to Virginia she would be re-enslaved." In Jefferson's "Head and Heart" letter, "Head" argues, "Everything in this world is matter of calculation. Advance then with caution, the balance in your hand. Put into one scale the pleasures which any object may offer; but put fairly into the other the pains which are to follow, and see which preponderates." Sally did just that.

Faced with those two futures, "she refused to return with him." She had the strength to choose freedom. That decision shows that she could envision a future in Paris, perhaps alongside her brother, who was a respected chef and could have supported them. Jefferson then made a better offer: if she came back, she would have "extraordinary privileges," and he made a "solemn pledge that her children should be freed at the age of twenty-one years." Family, home, a better life, and freedom for her children: Sally agreed.

For Jefferson, bringing Sally, their unborn child, and James back represented a way to resolve all of his conflicts. He would be true to his vow to Martha, yet have a beautiful woman by his side. He could see himself as a good provider, caring for the Hemings family and preparing his mixed children for freedom. He still believed in liberty, in progress, but under his slow and careful guidance. If he treated those he owned well, trained his mixed-race children so that they could earn a living, eventually, someday, that inevitable wave of liberty, of freedom, would reach them. He could be a custodian, a parent, waiting for times to change and his children to grow up. Sally was not as willing to wait for fate.

Out of love for Jefferson, or the pleasure of being needed by him, or fear of the unknown, or the desire to be with her family, or some mixture of all of these, she would go back, but on her terms. Freedom was not a vague sense of historical destiny—it was a pledge, a commitment, a form of law.

If one side of the revolutionary year was high ideals and a second side was enslavement, for Jefferson and for Hemings a kind of resolution lay in family. Indeed, it was precisely the fact that they seemed so much like a married couple, a man and woman who were truly bonded, that bothered Jefferson's white critics. They could understand having an enslaved mistress, but not a true partnership across racial lines. "Why have you not married some worthy woman of your own color?" an irate writer demanded of Jefferson when he was president. The deep family bond, though, had profound consequences, which exposes the fatal flaw in Jefferson's image of plantation life.

Jefferson saw himself as a biblical patriarch providing a great umbrella of family for all, his relations and his property. This was a fantasy, which relied on an image of an owner as perfectly good and on enslaved people as willing to remain in his care as perpetual children. It ignored a reality that the story of the Hemingses, the Wayleses, and the Jeffersons makes crystal clear: no matter what white people claimed about race purity, they formed families with Africans—families they treated as ghosts. The damage of slavery was not just the brutalization of African Americans; it was the hardening of the hearts of white Americans. White men lived in a schizophrenic reality in which they denied, ignored, even sold their lovers, their own children. A white wife needed to pretend she did not notice the children growing up nearby and playing with her own children, enslaved children who resembled her husband, their father. "Any lady," Mary Boykin Chesnut, wife of a southern planter, wrote in her diary, "is able to tell who is the father of all the mulatto children in everybody's household but their own. Those she seems to think drop from the clouds." The reality of blended families and the lie of slavery left scars on the backs of African Americans and the souls of white Americans.

Sally embraced a life embedded among those she loved, with a guarantee of her children's freedom. This was a far more practical idea than Jefferson's. She strengthened her bonds of affection now and built her children's future on the foundation of a firm promise, which Jefferson indeed fulfilled. He chose love and dreams; she chose love and law. In that revolutionary year, ideas and ideals, enslavement and love, were all bound together for them to live, and for us to try to understand.

"ALL MEN ARE CREATED EQUAL"

THE GLOBAL JOURNEY OF OLAUDAH EQUIANO

JOYCE HANSEN

I *WAS BORN* in the year 1745, situated in a charming, fruitful vale, named Essaka. The distance of this province from the capital of Benin and the sea coast must be very considerable, for I had never heard of white men or Europeans, nor of the sea. . . . "Thus begins the quiet opening of one man's story that shocked many who read it in 1789, the first year it was published.

Using his words to create powerful images, Olaudah Equiano, a forty-four-year-old African living in London, introduced his readers to the world of enslavement in his autobiography, *The Interesting Narrative of the Life of Olaudah Equiano, or Gustavus Vassa, the African, Written by Himself.* His autobiographical narrative would become a powerful tool of the British anti-slavery movement. One writer called it a "runaway best seller." Over three hundred members of the British aristocracy, including members of Parliament, were the first to read the narrative when it was published. They certainly knew about slavery—many benefited economically from the trade. But they knew about it from a safe distance. Olaudah's words drew his readers inside a slaver (a ship used to transport slaves) and inside the hearts and minds of flesh-and-blood people, in a way that no anti-slavery lecture or pen-and-ink illustration could do.

> *The first object which saluted my eyes when I arrived on the coast, was the sea, and a slave ship . . . waiting for its cargo. These filled me with astonishment, which was soon converted into terror, when I was carried on board. I was immediately handled, and tossed up to see if I were sound, by some of the crew; and I was now persuaded that I had gotten into a world of bad spirits, and that they were going to kill me. Their complexions, too, differing so much from ours, their long hair, and the language they spoke (which was very different from any I had ever heard), united to confirm me in this belief. . . .*
>
> *When I looked round the ship too, and saw a large furnace of copper boiling, and a multitude of black people of every description chained together, every one of their countenances expressing dejection and sorrow, I no longer doubted of my fate; and, quite overpowered with horror and anguish, I fell motionless on the deck and fainted.*

In his opening chapter, Olaudah described the culture that nourished him, the people who loved him, and the future that awaited him when he would become an important chief like his father. That future ended when he was eleven years old.

> *One day when all our people were gone out to their works as usual, and only I and my dear sister were left to mind the house, two men and a woman got over our walls, and in a moment seized us both,*

and, without giving us time to cry out, or make resistance, they
stopped our mouths, and ran off with us into the nearest wood.
Here they tied our hands, and continued to carry us as far as they
could, till night came on, when we reached a small house, where
the robbers halted for refreshment, and spent the night. . . .

The next day proved a day of greater sorrow than I had yet
experienced; for my sister and I were then separated, while we
lay clasped in each other's arms. It was in vain that we besought
them not to part us; she was torn from me, and immediately carried
away. . . . I cried and grieved continually; and for several days did
not eat anything but what they forced into my mouth.

Olaudah doesn't tell us how old his sister was but referred to her
as his playmate, so they were probably close in years. He said that he
changed masters many times, passed from hand to hand from one
village to another and one family to the next, until he reached the
coast and saw the sea, and the slave ship waiting for its cargo.

Traditionally, in some West African countries, slavery had been
used as a punishment for committing a crime. People captured in
wars might also be enslaved. At times, captives might either be freed
after a certain period or integrated into the society or ethnic group
where they had been held as slaves. Children weren't kidnapped and
sold like pieces of hot goods. Olaudah explained that he was moved
from one African village to another and in a few cases stayed with
families. Many things, including language, were familiar to him. That
all changed when he reached the coast.

The insatiable European demand for slave labor in their colonies in the Caribbean and North and South America, and the African
chiefs and kings who supplied the slaves in exchange for weapons
that gave them power and control over their neighbors, helped to
create the Atlantic slave trade that plagued the continent from the

seventeenth to the nineteenth century. The nature of African slavery had changed by the time Olaudah and his sister were kidnapped.

Yet, even though he was caught in this web, a wonderful thing happened to Olaudah. "I had been travelling for a considerable time, when, one evening, to my great surprise, whom should I see brought to the house where I was but my dear sister! As soon as she saw me she gave a loud shriek, and ran into my arms . . . neither of us could speak . . . unable to do anything but weep. . . . For a while we forgot our misfortunes, in the joy of being together."

Their joy was short-lived. They were separated again the next day. One of the most heart-wrenching passages in his narrative is Olaudah's fears of what might have happened to his sister. "I was now more miserable, if possible, than before. The small relief which her presence gave me from pain was gone, and the wretchedness of my situation was redoubled by my anxiety after her fate, and my apprehensions lest her sufferings be greater than mine, when I could not be with her to alleviate them. . . . Though you were early forced from my arms, your image has been always riveted in my heart."

Olaudah was sold two more times after his sister was taken away, and he arrived in the coastal region of West Africa about seven months after they had been kidnapped. He never saw her again. It's estimated that about 12.5 million Africans made the same trek to the West African coast as Olaudah and, possibly, his sister.

Anti-slavery drawings and illustrations were often used by abolitionists in Britain to show the horrors of slavery—a slave on his knees with his wrists tied, a slave being whipped, a slave hanging by his ribs. But when we read Olaudah's words and imagine his voice as he writes about the joys of his childhood and the cruel separation from his sister, we are with a human being like ourselves. We are not looking at an artist's version of imagined events. Olaudah didn't imagine this reality. He lived it and made his readers feel it.

A drawing couldn't re-create the smells, the cries, the suffering in a mother's eyes.

One of the most iconic depictions of a slave vessel at the time of Olaudah's narrative was a print of the eighteenth-century British ship *Brookes*. Captives were packed in just inches apart. In 1788, a year before Olaudah's publication, a British anti-slavery organization used an illustration of the plan of this ship to show Parliament that the *Brookes* and similar vessels were carrying more people than they were designed to accommodate. The vessel became a symbol of this inhumane practice and was a frequent illustration in anti-slavery publications. We look at the familiar image and wonder how people remained chained just inches apart during a lengthy voyage. Olaudah gave us more than an image.

I was soon put down under the decks, and there I received such a salutation in my nostrils as I had never experienced in my life: so that, with the loathsomeness of the stench, and crying together, I became so sick and low that I was not able to eat, nor had I the least desire to taste anything. I now wished for the last friend, death, to relieve me; but soon, to my grief, two of the white men offered me eatables; and, on my refusing to eat, one of them held me fast by the hands, and laid me across . . . the windlass, and tied my feet, while the other flogged me severely. . . .

The stench of the hold while we were on the coast was so intolerably loathsome, that it was dangerous to remain there for any time, and some of us had been permitted to stay on the deck for the fresh air; but now that the whole ship's cargo were confined together, it became absolutely pestilential. The closeness of the place, and the heat of the climate, added to the number in the ship, which was so crowded that each had scarcely room to turn himself, almost suffocated us. This produced copious perspirations so that the air soon became unfit for respiration, from a variety of loathsome smells, and brought on a sickness among the slaves, of which many died. . . . This wretched situation was again aggravated by the filth of the necessary tubs [filled with human waste], into which the children often fell, and were almost suffocated. The shrieks of the women, and the groans of the dying, rendered the whole scene of horror almost inconceivable. . . .

One day, when we had a smooth sea and moderate wind, two of my wearied countrymen who were chained together . . . preferring death to such a life of misery, somehow made through the nettings and jumped into the sea; immediately, another quite dejected fellow . . . also followed their example.

Olaudah's journey across the Atlantic Ocean lasted approximately two months. The first land he saw was the island of Barbados in the Caribbean. The ship docked at its capital, Bridgetown. He described the merchants and planters rushing on board. The Africans were put into groups with the men separated from the women and children; most humiliating of all, their potential buyers examined every part of their bodies as if they were beasts of burden.

As Olaudah showed us, there seemed to be no sense among the men who traded and purchased Africans that they were dealing with human beings who could feel pain and suffering.

I remember, in the vessel in which I was brought over, in the men's apartment, there were several brothers, who, in the sale, were sold in different lots; and it was very moving on this occasion, to see and hear their cries at parting. . . . Why are parents to lose their children, brothers their sisters, or husbands their wives? Surely, this is

a new refinement in cruelty, which, while it has no advantage to
atone for it, thus aggravates distress, and adds fresh horrors even
to the wretchedness of slavery.

How could Olaudah's contemporary readers, witnessing in 1789 the clamoring of Europeans and Americans of all stripes for individual rights, read Olaudah's narrative and not be moved to feel something, to say something, to do something?

Olaudah stayed on Barbados for a short time with others who weren't purchased—perhaps they were too sickly, or too old, or like Olaudah too young and slight. He was put on a plantation for about two weeks, he said, weeding grass and gathering stones. "I stayed in this island for a few days, I believe it could not be above a fortnight, when I and some few more slaves, that were not saleable amongst the rest, from very much fretting, we were shipped off in a sloop for North America."

Olaudah was brought to the estate of the Virginia man who had purchased him. He was ordered to fan his owner, Mr. Chambers, who was ill. He was frightened and confused when he entered the home. Everything was so strange. "I had seen a black woman slave . . . who was cooking the dinner, and the poor creature was cruelly loaded with various kinds of iron machines; she had one particularly on her head, which locked her mouth so fast that she could scarcely speak; and could not eat nor drink. I was much astonished and shocked at this contrivance, which I afterwards learned was called the iron muzzle." His readers must have been shocked as well. This was happening in a gentleman's house—not on a slave ship.

Olaudah doesn't say how long he was in the home, but he was there long enough to learn a few words of English and to have his name changed. He was called Jacob. Eventually, a lieutenant of the Royal Navy, Michael Henry Pascal, purchased him.

When he left Virginia with Pascal, he was forced to change his name again. "While I was on board this ship, my captain and master named me Gustavus Vassa. I at this time began to understand him a little, and refused to be called so, and told him as well as I could that I would be called Jacob; but he said I should not, and still called me Gustavus: and when I refused to answer to my new name, which I at first did, it gained me many a cuff; so at length I submitted, and by which I have been known ever since."

Olaudah was enslaved to Pascal for about ten years. He became a skilled seaman, serving mainly on ships. He was also determined to learn how to read and write. Olaudah obtained religious instruction and became a devout Christian. He was baptized in St. Margaret's Church in Westminster, London, in 1759, over his master's objections—Pascal didn't want Christianity to get in the way of slavery. The crew of one of the ships he worked on called him the black Christian.

He remained enslaved, but he never ceased trying to figure out ways to attain his freedom. He even paid a crew member on one of the ships where he served to show him how to navigate. Shipboard life in the eighteenth century was mean and brutal. His heart ached every time he worked on a ship carrying "live cargo," meaning slaves. As Olaudah recounted his experiences at sea, he spoke to the reader about the injustices he observed around him. Women and girls were especially brutalized.

> . . . it was almost a constant practice with our clerks, and other whites, to commit violent depredations on the chastity of the female slaves; and these I was, though with reluctance, obliged to submit to at all times, being unable to help them. When we have had some of these slaves on board my master's vessels, to carry them to other islands, or to America, I have known our mates to commit these

acts most shamefully, to the disgrace, not of Christians only, but of men. I have even known them to gratify their brutal passion with females not ten years old; and these abominations, some of them practiced to such scandalous excess, that one of our captains discharged the mate and others on that account.

Olaudah was also appalled by the way enslaved people were treated in the Caribbean.

These overseers are indeed for the most part persons of the worst character of any denominations of men in the West Indies. . . . [G]entlemen . . . not residing on their estates, are obliged to leave the management of them in the hands of these human butchers, who cut and mangle the slaves in a shocking manner on the most trifling occasions, and altogether treat them in every respect like brutes. They pay no regard to the situation of pregnant women, nor the least attention to the lodging of the field Negroes. Their huts, which ought to be well covered, and the place dry where they take their little repose, are often open sheds, built in damp places; so that when the poor creatures return from the toils of the field, they contract many disorders, from being exposed to the damp air in this uncomfortable state.

Olaudah always reminded himself that he was a Christian and had been baptized; therefore he was free. He freed himself in his own mind first, and when he turned twenty-one years old, he confronted his owner.

"I told him I was free, and he could not by law serve me so." Pascal was so enraged that he sold Olaudah. But Olaudah's assertion of freedom in the end led to his liberation. He was sold to Robert King of Philadelphia—a merchant and a Quaker. The Quakers had an uneasy relationship with slavery. For the most part, Quakers were considered to be anti-slavery; however, the slave system was so much a part of trading and doing business that a successful Quaker merchant would employ slave labor.

Olaudah served with a Captain Doran, who handled King's shipping business. The captain gave Olaudah the opportunity to earn a bit of money, buying and selling small amounts of merchandise, and in three years he earned enough money to purchase his own freedom. Forty pounds sterling it cost him to be once more in his "original free African state," as Olaudah said. He purchased his freedom from Robert King on July 11, 1766—ten years before the American Declaration of Independence.

For the next eleven years, he continued working as a seaman. Though he was free, he never forgot his fellow Africans still held in slavery. He published anti-slavery articles in London newspapers and was one of the signers of an anti-slavery petition presented to Queen Charlotte, wife of King George III. He also attempted to obtain an appointment from the bishop of London to work as a missionary in Africa. He was not successful, but he was asked by the government to supervise the supplies needed for an expedition to resettle Africans living in England to Sierra Leone. The expedition did not materialize; Olaudah never returned to Africa.

It would be his autobiographical narrative that resonated and had the most impact, not only when it was first published, but for generations afterward. The scholar and writer Charles T. Davis said that Olaudah's narrative "is a respected forerunner of the slave accounts that began to appear in the 1830s." Olaudah's autobiography was reprinted in nine editions and translated into Dutch, German, and Russian. He sold almost two thousand copies of the narrative when he visited Ireland in 1791. A reviewer said that Olaudah was a "principal instrument in bringing about the motion for a repeal of the Slave-Act." Another commentator, a white abolitionist, credited Olaudah with being "more use to the Cause [anti-slavery] than half the People in the country."

The old order in western Europe was changing in 1789; ordinary people—servants, laborers, farmers, peasants, craftsmen—demanded the right to have control over their own lives. They could rule themselves, they said, and did not need noblemen and aristocrats controlling them. Parisians stormed the Bastille prison, a symbol of the power and brutality of the French monarchy. The French Revolution would follow. A new order began to take root.

The Americans had already declared, thirteen years earlier, that all men were created equal. In 1789 they wrote the Bill of Rights, the first ten amendments to their Constitution, protecting individual liberties and ensuring that citizens would not be terrorized by a powerful government—not even a government of their own creation.

Yet in the midst of these cries for individual liberty and human rights, chattel slavery remained the reality for millions of Africans brought to the West. Olaudah Equiano knew their plight firsthand. He gave his enslaved African brothers and sisters a voice they didn't have in this year of 1789, when Americans and Europeans were demanding equality and liberty. Slavery in America, however, did not end until 1865.

Olaudah's autobiographical narrative is a testament to the idea that every person has the right to be free—the same idea expressed by those eighteenth-century men and women who tried to throw off the chains of powerful monarchies and oppressive governments. Olaudah knew about chains.

Some pro-slavery advocates said that Olaudah was not born in Africa, but in South Carolina. Others claimed that he was born in Saint Croix, a Danish colony in the Caribbean. Olaudah denied these charges and offered as proof that he was born in Africa the testimony of people, still living, who remembered him when he first came to London and barely spoke English.

Despite those who questioned his authenticity and people who still question whether he was born in Africa, we do know that Olaudah was not a fictional character. He had been on slavers whether or not he was born in Africa, and he would have witnessed slavery in the Caribbean and in America. A scholar writing in the 1990s, researching records from the British Royal Navy, verified much of the information in Olaudah's narrative.

I believe that Olaudah Equiano, or Gustavus Vassa, not only wanted to tell the story of his life, but also wanted to declare along with his contemporaries, white and black, the immorality and inhumanity of slavery. He had no idea that his autobiography would be read centuries after its first printing and that his voice, his thoughts, and his heartfelt desire for liberty for himself and others would still speak to people as we continue to grapple with issues related to human and individual rights.

What does freedom of speech, religion, and the press mean to us in the twenty-first century? How do we interpret the right to bear arms in our generation? How do we confront and stop human trafficking and other forms of modern slavery? We must keep our voices raised against injustice and never forget, as Olaudah has shown us, that all men and women are created equal.

INSPI

WHAT penalty will we impose on Louis? . . . For myself, I abhor the death penalty lavishly imposed by your laws, and I feel neither love nor hatred for Louis; I hate only his crimes. I have asked for the abolition of the death penalty . . . it can be justified only in cases where it is necessary to the safety of individuals or society. But Louis must die because the homeland must live.

—MAXIMILIEN DE ROBESPIERRE, 1793, in a speech given before the National Convention in Paris. A leading member of the Committee of Public Safety, Robespierre encouraged the execution of more than 17,000 men and women who were condemned as enemies of the revolution. Robespierre was sent to the guillotine the next year.

LET us arm ourselves, we have the right to do so by nature and by law. Let us show men that we are not inferior, either in virtue or in courage.

—THÉROIGNE DE MÉRICOURT, 1792, in a speech calling for the formation of female regiments. An organizer and activist during the French Revolution, Méricourt believed that women deserved equal rights, including the right to be armed. Her brother committed her to an asylum in 1795.

TION

BUT the rights of men result simply from the fact they are rational, sentient beings, susceptible of acquiring ideas of morality, and of reasoning concerning those ideas. Women having, then, the same qualities, have necessarily the same rights.

— *MARIE-JEAN-ANTOINE-NICOLAS DE CARITAT,*
Marquis de Condorcet, 1790. In a newspaper article, the French
philosopher of the Enlightenment drew attention to the fact that the
National Assembly in France failed to include women's rights and
educational reform for women. Although women didn't win the right
to vote during the French Revolution, they did win changes in matters
of marriage, divorce, inheritance, and custodial rights of children.
Women later lost many of these rights during Napoléon's reign.

THE WESLEYANS
IN THE
WEST INDIES

SUMMER EDWARD

O N JULY 28, 1789, at the annual Methodist conference in Britain, a Welshman stood up and began speaking. He had come to plead the case of the enslaved Africans in the West Indies, as the Caribbean islands were then called. He had long been zealous about the "salvation" of enslaved people and had spent the previous year going from door to door begging assistance for the establishment of Methodist missions on the islands. This man was Dr. Thomas Coke, one of the first appointed bishops of the Methodist Church. His appeal was so ardent and convincing that by the end of the British conference, he had gained the overwhelming support of the assembly.

Coke was not alone in his convictions. In 1789, a year of worldwide social reforms and upheaval, many Methodists living in England were proactive abolitionists who publicized slavery's evils. Whites who converted to Methodism had to emancipate their slaves or else face expulsion from the church. "When shall the Sun of

Righteousness arise on these outcasts of men, with healing in His wings!" John Wesley, a British priest, once bemoaned, referring to black slaves. Fifty years before, Wesley, the Oxford-educated son of a religious nonconformist, had started a revival movement within the Church of England that had led to the development of Methodism. Because of him, the early Methodist preachers who made their way to the West Indies were also called "Wesleyans."

Methodism's anti-slavery stance was not its only challenge to accepted beliefs of the day. Unlike many other Protestant denominations, Methodists rejected the idea that only certain people have been "elected" by God to receive salvation and eternal life. Instead, the early Methodists proclaimed that all people have the opportunity to be saved through faith in Jesus Christ. Another distinctive feature of early Methodism was its systematic use of "methods" and "rules" in conducting religious affairs. At the same time, the early Methodists' emotional worship and dramatic open-air preaching to working-class people, criminals, and others who were ostracized by organized religion distinguished them from the Church of England, the centuries-old established state church of Britain. Finally, Methodism shook up established religious thinking by training ordinary laypeople to lead the majority of religious services as opposed to ordained clergy; thus, in its inception, Methodism was a grassroots movement led by folk theologians intent on speaking plain truth to all people.

The Gospel for All People

John Wesley had always stressed the far-reaching inclusivity of the Gospel; as a young man, the same year he founded Methodism, he penned these oft-quoted words: "I look upon all the world as my parish; thus far I mean, that, in whatever part of it I am, I judge it meet, right, and my bounden duty, to declare unto all that are willing to hear, the glad tidings of salvation."

Wesley spent much of 1789 publicly refuting the idea that the Methodist Church had turned its back on the Church of England, otherwise known as the Anglican Church. The fact is, Wesley was a staunch opponent of separatism in all its forms. He and his true supporters wanted "to stir up all parties, Christians or Heathens, to worship God in spirit and in truth."

Right across the Channel, the French Revolution had just begun, and the escalating cries of *"liberté, égalité, fraternité!"* must have greatly comforted an aged Wesley in his twilight years. A ground-breaking civil rights document, the Declaration of the Rights of Man and of the Citizen, was also published in France in 1789, recognizing that all "men are born free and equal" without exception. With these daring ideas spreading like wildfire and stirring up debate across the globe, the early Methodists set sail for the slave colonies of the West Indies.

Bishop Dr. Coke: Methodist Missions Start-Up Guy

Affectionately dubbed "the flea" by Wesley because he "hopped" about tirelessly doing the work of God, Dr. Thomas Coke would go down in history as the "Father of Methodist Missions," an indomitable maverick, well suited to his role as superintendent of Methodism's overseas missions. Indeed, it was Coke, a devoted assistant to Wesley, who persistently entreated the latter until he finally gained permission to send missionaries to the West Indies. Dr. Coke used his skills as a negotiator to petition other bishops and influential British statesmen for funding and personnel for missionary work in the West Indies.

Methodism Arrives in the Caribbean

In the years prior to 1789, Methodism had already begun to take root in the West Indies. In the second half of the eighteenth century, a number of Methodists immigrated to the island colonies and had already opened their homes to Methodist worship before Dr. Coke arrived. It was Dr. Coke, however, who arrived in the West Indies in 1789 bearing the official mandate for methodical (the very quality that earned Methodists their name) missionary work in the islands. In the two years prior, Coke had made exploratory trips with fellow missionaries to Antigua, Dominica, Saint Vincent, Saint Kitts, Nevis, Barbados, and Saint Eustatius, and they had met infant churches in many of the colonies.

According to Coke's journal, during his travels in 1789, he found the work of God spreading swiftly among the black inhabitants of the West Indies, whom he described as "delightful" and "tranquil" and praised as being "simple-hearted." Ironically, this stereotype of enslaved people as docile and childlike reflects the same patronizing, paternalistic attitudes harbored by those whites who justified slavery.

In the West Indies, Coke and his supporters from the United Kingdom and North America built Methodist chapels and school-rooms and preached the Gospel to blacks, whites, and indigenous Amerindian peoples alike. Coke organized groups of churches into traveling circuits, gathered the scattered flock into societies, and provided for their religious instruction. In each island he visited, he left behind preachers and appointed mission leaders, as well as scores of converted souls. By the middle of 1789, the Methodist following in the islands numbered in the thousands, and there were mission stations in Antigua, Saint Kitts, Nevis, Tortola, Saint Eustatius, Saba, Jamaica, Barbados, Dominica, Saint Vincent, and Grenada.

Men, Devils, and the Persecuting Spirit
On January 19, 1789, a passage boat docked at Port Royal, Jamaica. Among the passengers who disembarked was Dr. Coke. The man who greeted him warmly and at whose house he lodged was one Mr. Fishley, a master shipwright in Her Majesty's royal dockyard and a

Wesleyan himself. It's likely, though not certain, that Dr. Coke led a small cottage service at Mr. Fishley's home at Port Royal (dubbed in the late 1600s as the "wickedest city on earth") before journeying to Kingston Harbour, where his first sermon in Jamaica is officially recorded as taking place.

In Jamaica Dr. Coke's efforts to remedy "the immense mass of heathenism" and "the gross darkness which covered the minds of the people" were met with stark, and often violent, opposition by members of the white ruling class. An extract from Dr. Coke's journal details an "unhappy incident" that occurred during a revival meeting:

> *The second evening, the great room, and all the piazzas round it, were crowded with people. I believe there were four hundred white people present (the largest number of Whites I ever preached to in the West Indies), and about two hundred Negroes; there being no room, I think, for more. After I had preached about ten minutes, a company of gentlemen, inflamed with liquor, began to be very turbulent; till at last the noise increasing, they cried out, "Down with him, down with him." They then pressed forwards through the crowd in order to seize me, crying out again, "Who seconds that fellow!" On which my new and gallant friend, Mr. Bull, whose house was then my residence, stepped forth between the rioters and me, saying, "I second him, against men and devils."... [A lady also] stood up, and reasoned boldly with the rioters on the impropriety of their conduct.*
>
> *Chagrined at the reproofs ... their activity began to lessen; and shame, the companion of conscious guilt, soon led them to desist from their design.*

Indeed, throughout the West Indies, many white people resisted the Wesleyans' work. While en route to the islands, the Wesleyan missionaries were scandalized by drunken sailors who subjected them to vulgar taunts and sometimes stole their personal belongings. Once in the colonies, Methodist preachers had to contend with rude colonial governors and chief magistrates full of barely disguised acrimony. Missionaries were thrown into the common jail for preaching to the enslaved, for ministering in the houses of free mulattos (the term used for mixed-race people), or for simply shaking hands with black people. Missionaries "were frequently so hooted in the streets and ill-treated, by having dirt and other things thrown at them."

Many whites feared that enslaved people who gathered for chapel services were really plotting conspiracies and planning revolts, so the colonial assemblies passed resolutions that further restricted their freedom of assembly and made it difficult for missionaries to obtain the required preaching licenses. Enslaved people who were caught singing hymns, praying, or attending chapel were cruelly flogged by their masters, and by some accounts, those with strong Christian convictions were even hanged. George Stanbury, enslaved in Spanish Town, Jamaica, was one of many sent to a correction house for preaching to his friends and family. In certain colonies, white colonists who aligned with the Methodist cause were imprisoned and had their goods confiscated; some were even banished from their island.

Ushering in the Tide of Change
Why did the Wesleyans face such censure, opposition, and hostility from the white ruling class in the West Indies? The fact is the Christian education and religious care of black people posed a grave threat to the social order that was already ripe for overthrow in 1789. As a part of their biblical mandate, Methodists considered it their duty to use Jesus's ethical teachings to confront societal problems

like poverty, inequality, slavery, and prison reform. Some of their actions—such as performing the first slave marriages solemnized in the Caribbean and teaching enslaved people to read English— were revolutionary. In islands like Nevis, the Methodist Society was fully responsible for the education of formerly enslaved Africans.

Although many West Indian planters theoretically agreed that the enslaved needed pastoral care, in practice, they chafed at the Methodists' wholehearted devotion to the spiritual formation of black people. Slave owners only initially allowed it because they thought Christianity could be used as a tool of social control; they hoped that biblical verses such as "servants, be obedient to them that are your masters" would keep the enslaved loyal and docile. In this, the planters were sorely mistaken.

Actually, it was partly the Christianization of West Indian slaves that emboldened them to start a number of rebellions, both violent and nonviolent, during the Georgian era and certainly in the years after 1789. The Christian Gospel of peace and freedom fueled enslaved people's political aspirations and inspired them with ideas of their natural and political rights.

Back in Britain, pro-slavery advocates publicly argued that the process of Christianization of the enslaved would catalyze the abolishment of the slave trade upon which the entire economy of England depended. They accused Methodists of "a dangerous fanaticism, productive of the most fatal consequences," and condemned them for "preaching seditious doctrines," "baneful and pestilent tenets," "which endanger the security of the white inhabitants, by exciting the Negroes to disaffection and revolt." Methodists were compelled to write many letters and disquisitions defending their activities in the colonies. London abolitionists went to great pains to prove that missionaries never directly or actively incited slaves to insubordination.

The Enslaved Africans Speak of Methodism

Most firsthand accounts of enslaved people's reactions to the Methodist mission movement come from journals, letters, and books written by white missionaries and other white observers. These accounts often focused on enslaved Africans' strong and mysterious reactions to Methodist sermons. Dr. Coke documented one experience in his journal: "The poor slaves were so affected under the word, that many of them fell down as if they were dead, and some of them would remain in a state of stupor for some hours."

Mary Prince, who escaped slavery in Bermuda and went to England to work as a paid servant, described her first experience of attending a Methodist prayer meeting in her slave narrative, *The History of Mary Prince*:

> *While we were at Date Hill Christmas came; and the slave woman who had the care of the place (which then belonged to Mr. Roberts the marshal), asked me to go with her to her husband's house, to a Methodist meeting for prayer, at a plantation called Winthorps. I went; and they were the first prayers I ever understood. One woman prayed; and then they all sung a hymn; then there was another prayer and another hymn; and then they all spoke by turn of their own griefs as sinners. The husband of the woman I went with was a black driver. His name was Henry. He confessed that he had treated the slaves very cruelly; but said that he was compelled to obey the orders of his master. He prayed them all to forgive him, and he prayed that God would forgive him. He said it was a horrid thing for a ranger to have sometimes to beat his own wife or sister; but he must do so if ordered by his master.*
>
> *I felt sorry for my sins also. I cried the whole night, but I was too much ashamed to speak. I prayed to God to forgive me. This*

meeting had a great impression on my mind, and led my spirit to
the Moravian church, so that when I got back to town, I went and
prayed to have my name put down in the Missionaries' book; and I
followed the church earnestly every opportunity. I did not then tell
my mistress about it; for I knew that she would not give me leave to
go. But I felt I must *go.*

Olaudah Equiano was an erudite poet who gained his freedom
from slavery and traveled throughout the West Indies, eventually
becoming an influential Methodist abolitionist. He wrote extensively
about his profound Christian conversion experience at the hands
of Methodist preachers. In his poem "Miscellaneous Verses," written
for a white readership, he bemoaned his life of sorrow and pain as a
slave for several stanzas, before describing Jesus Christ as his great
emancipator:

Like some poor pris'ner at the bar,
Conscious of guilt, of sin and fear,
Arraign'd, and self-condemned, I stood—
"Lost in the world and in my blood!"

Yet here, 'midst blackest clouds confin'd,
A beam from Christ, the day-star, shin'd:
Surely, thought I, if Jesus please,
He can at once sign my release.

Even when they were as impressively gifted as Equiano, black
Methodists in the West Indies were not officially allowed to preach,
exhort, or proselytize until the mid-1800s, but with the support of
Dr. Coke and other white missionaries, a number of them rose to

unofficial positions of authority within their societies and circuits before then. Among the enslaved and free people of color who led Methodist societies without official denominational approval were Sarah Ann Gill, a free mulatta in Barbados; Mary "Mother" Wilkinson, a free mulatta woman who performed lay slave marriages in Jamaica; Robert James, an enslaved Jamaican who "hired himself from his owner in order to find time for doing good"; and Sophia Campbell and Mary Alley, who both hosted meetings in their cottages in Antigua.

Throughout the British West Indies, segregated seating at churches persisted until well after emancipation in 1833, with separate pews and galleries at the back reserved for people of color. Moreover, white Methodists did not believe that black people could effectively run their own churches and swiftly took control of any black Methodist churches that were started, quashing their attempts at independence.

Historical evidence overwhelmingly points to the fact that most of the enslaved favored converting to Methodism or other forms of Christianity; however, very little of the history of Methodism has been written or published by enslaved people themselves, so it is difficult to know the full extent of their true thoughts about Christianization. Through Christianization, enslaved people could become educated and make progress toward equality. Women relied on missionaries and ministers for protection from their masters' sexual exploitations. Importantly, Methodism also afforded the enslaved hope: the promise of a glorious and rewarding afterlife was a great source of comfort for those subjected to an earthly life of toil and suffering.

Spirituality Lessons: Then and Now
It is tempting to say that Christianization did the enslaved nothing but good, but that would be missing the bigger picture. Before the

arrival of Christian missionaries, enslaved people in the Caribbean had secretly practiced their African tribal religions and developed new syncretic religions: Obeah and Myalism. When the enslaved relinquished their African religions, they also gave up a vital part of their cultural and tribal identities, and suffered the partial loss of invaluable indigenous knowledge systems and traditions. On the other hand, ironically, it is partly because of the slave trade that some of the gifts and powers of indigenous African spirituality have now made their way around the world.

When the French Declaration of the Rights of Man and of the Citizen was published in 1789, one of its articles stated: "No one may be disturbed for his opinions, even religious ones, provided that their manifestation does not trouble the public order established by the law." Early Christian missionaries were certainly "disturbed" by many who feared, resented, and opposed their peaceful and progressive work in the West Indies, but in planting the seeds of Christianity in the Caribbean, Methodists, Catholics, Anglicans, and other groups respected one another's differences and set the tone for the harmonious religious coexistence that continues in the Caribbean to this day.

The world back in 1789 was one in which enslaved people who embraced Methodism were thwarted on every side and atrociously persecuted for daring to claim the social and political status and protections afforded to Christians. Also, most enslaved people did not have the privilege of "shopping around" for the right religion that fit them like many of us do now; they simply found strength and hope in whatever denominational teachings were made available to them by their white owners. Today black Christians in the Caribbean can sit peacefully in racially integrated church pews, and attend whatever church they like, without fear of any negative repercussions. At a time when many countries are experiencing a rise in attacks on churches—acts of senseless violence driven by intolerance and racism—the Caribbean's ongoing record of religious tolerance and freedom is remarkable.

In 1789 John Wesley said no to separation—between different peoples and races, and between the Methodist Church and the Church of England. Although a formal split from the Church of England eventually occurred in 1795, historically the two faiths aren't that different; the Methodist Church sprang from the Church of England, which itself sprang from the Catholic Church. This raises the question—have all religions evolved from the religions that came before them? And if so, to paraphrase Mahatma Gandhi, are honest differences not a healthy sign of progress? Surely this is one of the many lessons we must glean as we look back at the history of the Wesleyans in the West Indies.

WHO COUNTED IN AMERICA?

THE BEGINNING OF AN ENDLESS CONVERSATION

CYNTHIA LEVINSON AND
SANFORD LEVINSON

*"When in the course of human events it becomes necessary for one people
to dissolve the political bands which have connected them with another . . ."*
—The Declaration of Independence

"We the People of the United States . . ."
—The Preamble to the Constitution

"Congress shall make no law . . . abridging . . . the right of the people . . ."
—The Bill of Rights

FROM OUR VERY BEGINNINGS, America's most stirring pronouncements have been made in the name of "the people." Government does not rest in the hands of a ruler, our founding documents argue. The people rule themselves.

Or, at least, that's what we like to think our founders meant. Actually, they never clarified exactly which "people" they had in mind, although they clearly made some assumptions as to who counted and who did not. They didn't even come to agreement on whether it was the people who ran the state governments or those at the national level who were the more important and influential leaders. Which "people" were to be recognized and whether we were to be a united country under an overarching government or a confederation of states are important questions that still remain with us today. In a sense, the Bill of Rights (as we know it today) best demonstrates these conflicts at the heart of our democracy.

The Year 1789 in the Upstart United States and in Venerable France
In 1789, inspired in part by the audacity of Americans who had declared their independence from the British crown, revolutionary leaders in France issued the Declaration of the Rights of Man and of the Citizen. Both the Declaration of Independence and the Declaration of Rights emphasized what has come to be called "popular sovereignty": rule by the people, limited by the duty to respect the "fundamental rights" of all people.

After the two countries overthrew their kings, statesmen set about rewriting the rules. Americans invented a form of representative government in which the citizenry elected the leadership. France's National Constituent Assembly, too, moved toward experiments in popular government.

Despite these common actions, however, the two countries were less similar than they might appear. Above all, the American Constitution established a system of both state and federal governments that tussled over which entity dominated the other. At the time, most Americans, including its new leadership, felt a primary loyalty to their home states—not to the nation. Our second president,

John Adams, said, "Massachusetts is our country," and Thomas Jefferson, our third president, declared, "Virginia, Sir, is my country."

The French Declaration of the Rights of Man, on the other hand, stated, "The principle of all sovereignty resides essentially in the nation." So, even though French people were very aware of regional differences—and even spoke regional languages—their primary loyalty was to the nation-state as a whole. These different perspectives led to a unitary, centralized government based in Paris, while a federal government was created on American soil, with powers shared—and, to this day, fought over—between the national and the state governments.

There were other differences between these two budding democracies. While both America and France considered "rights" important, each country had its own understandings of who was eligible for which kinds of rights. For instance, both declarations proclaimed "liberty" as fundamental. Thomas Jefferson even called it one of our "unalienable rights" that could not be taken away by any government. Nevertheless, slavery remained legal in most of the thirteen states that made up the Union.

This was not the case across the ocean, however. As America's ambassador to France during the run-up to the French Revolution, Jefferson knew that France did not allow slavery within the country. (French territories, such as Saint-Domingue, which was later called Haiti, were another matter.) Nevertheless, he brought enslaved people he owned with him to Paris and kept their status secret. (For more on this, see Marc Aronson's chapter, "The Choice: Paris, 1789.")

Thus, all men in France had similar rights, whereas the rights of men in America depended on whether or not they were enslaved. Moreover, unlike France, the United States had a substantial indigenous population on whom settlers from abroad—and their descendants—imposed a new political order. (See Christopher Turner's chapter, "Mary Jemison and the Seneca Nation: 1789.") The area where the two countries shared a common perspective was women's rights: in both countries, women remained largely powerless.

The US Constitution

The first political system that officially went into effect after the American Revolution was established by the Articles of Confederation and Perpetual Union in 1781. The arrangement maintained so much power at the state level and provided so little at the national level that, by 1787, Alexander Hamilton called the system "imbecility." A major problem was that the national Congress could not collect taxes. All it could do was issue requisitions to the states, which amounted to begging. In 1786 Congress pleaded for $3.8 million to pay off war debts. The states chipped in $663. As a result, the government couldn't pay the soldiers who had won the war. In retaliation, four hundred of these soldiers stormed the Congress's headquarters and locked the delegates inside.

To resolve the financial and other crises, a new constitution was called for, and over the summer of 1787, a total of fifty-five men gathered in Philadelphia to craft it. Behind the scenes—literally, since the doors were locked and the windows shuttered throughout the Constitutional Convention—the framers confronted a variety of dilemmas while crafting the mechanics of government. As is usually the case in conducting political negotiations, compromises proved necessary. One action that compromisers often take is to kick cans down the road so that other people will have to make the difficult decisions that were postponed earlier. The Constitution opened stirringly in the name of "We the People." Yet since there was little agreement on what that phrase meant, some of the most important can-kicking involved defining both who "We the People" were and what actual powers and rights they should have.

Despite their lofty language, the framers did not actually believe that ordinary folks were educated or thoughtful enough to make sensible laws or vote directly for the president. Elbridge Gerry, a delegate from Massachusetts, even said that the people are "dupes." This is one explanation for the fact that the Constitution of the United States—in contrast to many later state constitutions—provides no way for the people themselves to participate in decision making, even in the process of ratifying the Constitution. *Everything* is done through "representatives." So, in many important ways, only elected officials "count" because they're the only ones authorized to carry out the business of governing.

Congress is the most obvious example of representative government. Another important example is the Electoral College. Unlike the citizens of every other major democratic country in the world, Americans do not vote directly for their president. Instead, we vote for other people, literally the electors, who assume the power to choose the president.

When James Madison came up with this plan and the founders signed on to it, they had multiple reasons to devise it, in particular the likelihood that in a vast landscape with few newspapers, the people themselves would have little way to know anything about the various candidates. Their representatives at the state level, on the other hand, would be knowledgeable and make wise choices. As Madison said at the Constitutional Convention, under his proposed system, "the instances will be very rare in which an untrustworthy man will . . . [become] President of the United States." To this day it is even legal, though extremely uncommon, for "faithless electors" to vote for someone other than the popular winner within a state. Indeed, the way Electoral College votes are tallied means that the person who has won the most votes across the country has failed to become the president five times in our history—twice in this century alone. Thus, the will of the voters is not the same as the winner of the election.

Not only were all the delegates to the Constitutional Convention men, they were also all white and endowed with a measure of wealth. So, from the outset, these were the only sorts of persons invited to the table, the only ones who mattered. American Indians, except for the few who paid taxes, were not considered at all. Women—other than unmarried females in New Jersey who owned property and could, therefore, vote until 1807—had no role in governance, either. Even if a (very) few men were sympathetic to women or others who had been excluded, almost no one cared enough to refuse to sign or ratify a constitution that ensured rule by rich white men.

Although several states allowed free black men to vote in state elections, these men had no voice at the national level. And the new Constitution gave states the power to deny them the right to vote. Just as New Jersey eliminated suffrage for women in 1807, North Carolina, which had allowed free blacks to vote, took away this right in the state constitutional convention of 1835, by a vote of 66–61. Even worse, the Constitution's three-fifths clause meant that this fraction of enslaved people—referred to as "other persons"—was added to the number of white people to determine how many representatives "slave states" could send to the lower house of Congress. This formula added significantly to the number of representatives allotted to Virginia, for example. Furthermore, since the size of each state's membership in the Electoral College equals the sum of its senators and representatives, slave states also got a boost when casting votes for presidents.

The first US Census, conducted in 1790, counted 700,000 enslaved persons, expanding these states' populations by 420,000 for these purposes. But, of course, those who were enslaved couldn't choose those representatives, let alone their president. And although some representatives opposed slavery, they did little to stop Congress from passing the 1793 Fugitive Slave Act, which required "free states" to return any enslaved persons who had tried to escape from their bondage. These enslaved people were identified as persons in the census but their value, both financially and politically, accrued to their owners. They counted only numerically.

American Indians were also not viewed as true members of the American political community. During the Revolutionary War, many native nations had supported the British, their long-standing trading partners, in part because some American citizens were eager to move west and settle lands occupied and owned by the nations of American Indians. In fact, the United States was almost continually at war for its first century with one or another of these nations, whose numbers plummeted.

Nine states, the minimum number needed, ratified the Constitution by June 1788. Two more states—importantly, the large states of Virginia and New York—did so the following month. North Carolina and Rhode Island, on the other hand, held out until well after George Washington's inauguration as the first president of the new political system on April 30, 1789. This date was more than six weeks after the official beginning of the new government on March 4. Since Washington's second term began on March 4, 1793, as mandated in the Constitution, he served slightly less than four years the first time he was in office. The odd length of Washington's first term exemplifies the practical difficulties in getting the government off the pages of the Constitution and into the solid realm of reality.

The Bill of Rights

The relative importance of the federal government versus the states affected the Bill of Rights. We often proudly proclaim the rights of Americans to free speech and freedom of religion, for instance. However, these rights are protected only by the federal government, not in the states.

Even before the Constitution was ratified, many people were bothered by something that was missing from the document. Unlike France's Declaration of the Rights of Man and of the Citizen, the US Constitution initially said almost nothing about what rights and liberties the populace would enjoy. At state ratifying conventions where the document was debated in 1788, some opponents focused on this absence. They accurately recognized that a far more power- ful national government was being created than had existed under the Articles of Confederation—critics described it as a "consolidated government"—which potentially threatened their freedom. These Anti-Federalists began to call for a "bill of rights" to protect the people from government overreach.

Federalist supporters of the Constitution, including James Wilson of Pennsylvania and Alexander Hamilton in New York, argued that a bill of rights was unnecessary because the new government had only the powers assigned to it. Why bother to enshrine a promise that people could own muskets, for instance, or practice whatever religion they wanted if the Constitution didn't say they couldn't? Furthermore, if a particular right was not included in the list, would that mean that it did not exist?

Previously, Representative James Madison of Virginia had also criticized proposals to protect specific rights. He called them "parch- ment barriers," not worth the paper they were written on, because Congress might simply ignore them. Madison changed his mind, however, possibly because he needed the support of voters who wanted such a bill when he was running for Congress, and possibly because they actually convinced him of the need.

On June 8, 1789, just three months after the First Congress convened, Madison proposed nineteen amendments to the Constitution. Among them was a bill of rights that would bar not only Congress but also state legislatures from passing laws that would limit people's freedom of conscience, speech, press, and assembly and the right to bear arms, among others.

Almost every other congressman opposed Madison's bill because they believed that the country's very first Congress faced more pressing issues than abstract concerns about "rights." As John Vining of Delaware explained, "The people are waiting with anxiety for the operation of the Government. . . . Let us not perplex ourselves by introducing one weighty and important question after another, till some decisions are made." Discussion of amendments was postponed in favor of setting up the "inferior courts" of the federal judiciary system and arguing where the nation's capital should be located.

Madison waited about six weeks, then begged the House "to indulge" him by considering his proposals. Not yet. Instead, they were shunted to a committee. A week later, the committee finally recommended consideration of Madison's amendments.

Nevertheless, many of his colleagues were suspicious. Referring to the often hopeless tactic used by harpooners to keep whales from attacking their fragile rowboats, Representative Aedanus Burke of South Carolina described Madison's proposals as "a tub thrown out to a whale." The "whale" here referred to politicians who wanted to hold a second Constitutional Convention at which they could weaken the national government and expand states' rights. Representative Thomas Tudor Tucker of South Carolina, for instance, urged, "It will be much better, I apprehend, to leave the state governments to themselves, and not to interfere with them more than we already do, and that is thought by many to be rather too much." A bill of rights would do nothing, they believed, to weaken the new national government, which they desperately wanted to do. The debate over this issue and over the need to protect individual rights altogether was so acrimonious that "a frequent call to Order became absolutely necessary."

Madison pleaded that his proposal dealing with state governments was "the most valuable amendment on the whole list; if there was any reason to restrain the government of the United States from infringing upon these essential rights, it was equally necessary that they should be secured against the state governments."

On August 24, 1789, the House voted to send seventeen of Madison's nineteen amendments to the Senate. Following more heated discussion, this body soundly rejected the notion of preventing states from passing laws against freedom of conscience, speech, and the press. Only the federal government would be prevented from restricting these rights. Anti-Federalists' fear of the national government combined with their relative trust in states help explain why the Bill of Rights limits actions only by the federal government. Madison completely failed in his efforts to include restrictions on *states*. The senators also decided to place amendments, if ratified, at the end of the Constitution instead of within the text itself, as Madison preferred. Grouped together, they acquired a collective identity, which we call the Bill of Rights, though they were rarely recognized as such at the time.

On September 25, 1789, Congress agreed on twelve amendments, which were sent to the states for ratification. By the end of the year, three states ratified various proposed amendments regarding individual rights, though it wasn't until 1791 that a total of ten amendments received necessary ratification to become part of the Constitution. (Thanks to the diligent research of a college student,

the original second amendment, which involved congressional sal-
aries, was added to the Constitution in 1992, thereby becoming the
Twenty-seventh Amendment, 203 years after it had been proposed!)

Despite his success in amending the Constitution, Madison was
bitterly disappointed that the document restricted only the national
government—not state governments—from taking away people's
liberties. After all, the text of what became the First Amendment
begins with the words "Congress shall make no law . . ." It says nothing about what states can't do. The French Declaration, in contrast,
applied to *all* levels of government. Madison realized this was not the
case in America, and the differences played out in many areas. One
of them related to compromises made with slave owners.

Were enslaved people part of "We the People" in whose name
the Constitution was ordained? Were their rights protected, at least
from the national government, by the Bill of Rights? How could they
be, unless one accepted the view that some persons could be bought,
owned, and sold by others—and that their children would auto-
matically become the property of their owners? The Fugitive Slave
Act, which Congress passed in 1793, was despised in some states
and lauded in others because it forced free states to return escaped
slaves. Ironically or not, some people interpreted the aspiration to
"establish justice," announced in the Preamble to the Constitution,
as being achieved by establishing national courts that would enforce
this terrible law.

The Constitution did not make clear who was a US citizen in
1789. Not even some of the framers themselves, such as Alexander
Hamilton, who was born on Nevis in the Leeward Islands, knew if
they counted as citizens. And what about immigrants? Did their land-
ing and residing in a state make them officially Americans? In 1790
Congress addressed the question of who was worthy of citizenship

by passing the country's first Naturalization Act, which limited naturalization to "a free white person . . . of good character." This law provided insight into whom Congress considered eligible and desirable
Americans; these did not include all immigrants, even if they had
been welcomed by a state.

There were also other areas where states and the national government were at odds in ways they could not be in France. The First
Amendment specifies, "Congress shall make no law respecting an
establishment of religion . . . or abridging the freedom of speech, or
of the press . . ." It did not limit the rights of states in these areas as
Madison had desired. For instance, Massachusetts continued to rec-
ognize Congregationalism as its established religion until 1833. Nor
did this amendment prevent that state from declaring blasphemy
illegal, as in this statute: "Whoever . . . by cursing or contumeliously
reproaching or exposing to contempt and ridicule, the holy word of
God contained in the holy scriptures shall be punished by impris-
onment in jail . . ." Congress could not pass a law against taking the
Lord's name in vain, but states could and did.

At the national level, too, Madison's fear that a bill of rights would
be mere "parchment barriers" seemed vindicated within a decade.
Even though the First Amendment guaranteed "freedom of speech,"
Congress passed the Sedition Act of 1798, which made it a crime to
show disrespect of the president in public. President John Adams was
only too happy to enforce it. Madison, by then a private citizen back in
Virginia, wrote a powerful critique of the law, and Thomas Jefferson
pardoned those convicted and jailed under it when he became president. But it took the Supreme Court until 1965 to state unequivocally
that the law was unconstitutional. In fact, until the twentieth century,
the Bill of Rights was rarely used to ensure the rights of any persons.
The Bill of Rights did not generally begin to apply to states until the
twentieth century, especially after World War II.

The Conversation Continues

The practical meaning of the various amendments that make up the Bill of Rights and the people to whom they apply inevitably change through time. Although some members of the Supreme Court insist that the "original meanings" of these rights should control decisions today, few people believe that these are knowable, let alone desirable. Even though the Eighth Amendment prohibits "cruel and unusual punishments," for instance, back in 1791, some states maimed convicted prisoners. Surely that would not happen today. But what about the death penalty—is it equally cruel? Similarly, the Fourth Amendment protects Americans from "unreasonable searches and seizures," which probably referred to officials entering and searching a home without a warrant in 1791. However, the phrase has taken on very different meanings in an age of cell phones, GPS devices, and lamppost cameras, which can track people's whereabouts.

The question of "personhood" also continues to be debated, partly because the Fourteenth Amendment, added to the Constitution in 1868, speaks about the rights of "persons," not just "citizens." This means that non-citizens, including undocumented aliens, have the same rights, laid out in the Bill of Rights, as citizens. Furthermore, the wording raises a conundrum about abortion. Is it a required constitutional *right*, as the Supreme Court held in 1973? Or is abortion *prohibited* by the Constitution because fetuses are constitutionally protected persons?

Constitutions—or declarations of rights—resolve only certain political issues, and even in doing so, they often raise others. A constitution might establish that representatives serve two-year terms or that presidents will be inaugurated on January 20. But debates about what it means to prevent governments from establishing a religion or abridging freedom of speech are ongoing.

MARY JEMISON
AND THE
SENECA NATION

1789

CHRISTOPHER TURNER

The Backdrop

THE AMERICAN REVOLUTION had been over, formally, for more than five years in 1789, and most white residents of North America understood their place in the new nation and had a sense of new opportunities for the future. For Native Americans, however, there was little to be confident about and no future that they could clearly see. The Treaty of Paris, which ended the Revolutionary War, had made no mention of their participation in the great war. Some in the new nation thought that this absence meant they were still at war with the Indians who had fought on both sides of the conflict, but mostly for the British. The treaty made peace between the United States and Britain, but it made no provision for recognizing Indian rights either as former allies of the British or in their future relations with the Americans.

In 1789, then, a sense of uncertainty pervaded communities such as the villages along Buffalo Creek on Lake Erie, where people from all across the land of the Haudenosaunee, the great Six Nations, had assembled and held tentative control. Most were refugees, all except some Seneca people for whom this was a traditional center of life. And for them, too, life with their brothers and cousins at such close hand, and in such destitute circumstances, was far from normal. One woman there, Mary Jemison, a Seneca elder, later dictated her life story. From her words, we can get a sense of what it was like for people to leave their homelands to the east, and the changes that would be required for them to survive alongside the newcomers, who were both the victors of the recent war and now their neighbors.

Mary Jemison

Mary Jemison's words were taken down, edited, and shaped by James E. Seaver, a doctor and minister who had researched the history of Native peoples in western New York during the Revolution. *A Narrative of the Life of Mrs. Mary Jemison* was published in 1824. Since Seaver's original notes did not survive, we will never know what he left out, added, or revised to make her life story suit his beliefs. But generations of careful scholars, as well as her descendants, believe that the real Mary comes through in the book. Based on her words and other research that fills in gaps, we can picture Mary on a spring morning in 1789. She might have looked up from her work planting corn seeds and gazed across a dramatic landscape. She would have seen a gorge hundreds of feet deep with the Genesee River running at its base surrounded by rich budding fields and, farther, woodland, with only a few cleared plots for cabins. She was in her forty-sixth year, though the sun had repeatedly tanned her skin over years and years of doing this same work, and she might have looked older. Based on her narrative, we can guess that Mary would not have been bitter in any way about the labor she did in the bright sunshine, but would have kept good thoughts in her mind as she did the important work of the first stage of nurturing the plants that would feed her five children, as well as the two men who toiled nearby building fences around the crops. She might well have remembered to thank the figures of "those that sustain us," spirits of the corn as well as the squash and the beans that would soon be growing up around her cornstalks, one plant nourishing the other. In order to keep these good thoughts at the forefront, though, she would have had to push aside other more troubling memories. After all, she could remember easily when the clearings of land with cabins were not there, and all the land around was the domain of her people, the Seneca Nation of Indians; for them, the fences had never been necessary.

And yet even this woman herself was not quite as she seemed. To the men who had recently come to work the land there with her, she was "Mary," but to her people, the Seneca, she was *Deh-he-wä-nis*, which meant "Two Falling Voices." Mary Jemison was her original name: she had been born in 1743 to a Scottish-Irish family while they were on a ship crossing over to America. The Jemisons settled on the Pennsylvania frontier, and when she was about fourteen years old, the family was caught up in the cross-currents of the Seven Years' War. Called the French and Indian War in American textbooks, this was a global contest between England and France, and both European powers had allies from Indian nations. In turn, the original Americans recognized colonists such as the Jemisons as a threat—people who were encroaching on long-established territories.

Mary was taken captive—often an Indian group that had lost a family member in battle would try to capture an enemy to adopt.

Indeed, Mary would eventually become fully adopted into the Seneca Nation, be given her name, and even have several children who were considered fully Seneca. Years later, after the end of the Seven Years' War and the American Revolution, she would be given the choice to return to what was by then the frontier of the new American nation. As Mary told Seaver, she already had a large family of her Seneca children. "If I should be so fortunate as to find my relatives," she said, "they would despise them, if not myself; and treat us as enemies; or, at least with a degree of cold indifference, which I thought I could not endure." She chose to remain a Seneca. Mary had already lived in many places, including the Ohio Valley, but in 1789, after many difficult years of conflict, she moved back to the upper Genesee River valley, among the Seneca relations of her husband who welcomed her to settle there. Still, things were changing very rapidly, and she had reason to worry for her children.

Mary could look east from her home across the greening Genesee River valley to where the "Long Knives," or Americans, were rapidly pushing toward her people's lands. The Seneca knew, all too well, what damage the Long Knives could cause, as they had experienced their full fury during the American Revolution.

For over a generation, Mary had served a key role in a chain of communications. She lived just off the main trails leading to the British fort at Niagara, which placed her along the western side of the Haudenosaunee frontier. There she received runners with messages and relayed the information to others who might come from the eastern nations such as the Cayuga and Onondaga. The Haudenosaunee were a confederacy of six nations that had agreed as far back as the 1400s (the date is uncertain) to govern themselves in a unique kind of democracy. In the 1770s, Benjamin Franklin recognized that the Haudenosaunee were an important model for the colonists. The six distinct groups agreed to abide by the Great Law of Peace, which was designed to make them strong together and to prevent conflict among them. A rare example of a true democracy that valued individual voices, the confederacy included the Seneca people Mary lived with in what is now western New York, and in the east, the Mohawk, in the valley still named for them. In between, there were the Oneida, Onondaga, Cayuga, and the Tuscarora; together they were the Six Nations Confederacy, or the Haudenosaunee, "People of the Longhouse."

The Haudenosaunee had formal trade and diplomatic relations with the British for well over a hundred years before the colonists began speaking of breaking away and forming their own nation. At first, then, most of the Haudenosaunee were inclined to stay out of the "family quarrel" between a father (King George) and his children (the colonists). But both the British and the rebels recognized that the Indian nations could be valuable allies—or dangerous enemies— and pressured them to take sides. Four of the six nations chose to rely on what was called "the Covenant Chain," a generations-old relationship of reciprocity and friendship, and support their longtime allies, the British. In 1777 Iroquois forces sided with the British, but then when hunting season began, they left to seek food for their families. By 1779, though, Iroquois warriors joined with British and Loyalist forces to attack settlements allied with the colonists.

General Washington realized the importance of the Indians to the outcome of the war and decided to make an assault on the Haudenosaunee a priority.

In the spring of 1779, Washington shifted a significant portion of his army to the north with the aim of devastating the Six Nations. He sent General John Sullivan into their country with specific orders to "cut off their settlements, destroy next year's crops, and do them every other mischief." The campaign was rapid, thoroughly destructive, and alarmingly effective. In just two months of marching through the interior of the Haudenosaunee country, Sullivan's army destroyed over forty villages, tens of thousands of bushels of crops, and thousands of fruit trees. Washington's instructions were clear—to "effect the complete devastation of their settlements." And that is precisely the "scorched earth" plan Sullivan executed.

Years later Mary would remember that invasion: "Our corn was good that year; a part of which we had gathered and secured for winter. . . . Sullivan and his army arrived at the Genesee river, where they destroyed every article of the food kind that they could lay their hands on . . . burning and destroying the huts and corn-fields; killing the cattle, hogs and horses, and cutting down the fruit trees." A decade later Mary still would have been able to see the charred evidence on trees and the edges of the woods all around her, and the damage to Little Beard's Town, across the river just within her view.

The ravages of Sullivan's march were only the beginning of a long hardship for the Seneca, as well as the Cayuga and Onondaga from the east. They began to flee west, to Fort Niagara on Lake Ontario. When the snows began to fall, deeper than any could remember, there were fewer and fewer animals to hunt, and the Cayuga and Onondaga turned to their former allies, the British. But there were too many of them; thousands from the two nations crowded around Fort Niagara in what could be seen as a vast refugee camp holding people devastated from the campaign and its violence. Without enough food to go around, they were forced to try to survive by eating anything, even boiling leather and making soup from mere bones. Many died, and sickness ravaged the camp through the next year. Mary might have recalled hearing a new name uttered around the bleak campfires by the fearful and shocked women, a name they would begin to use for General Washington and continue to use for every US president since: Hanadagá:yas, or "Town Destroyer."

Some Haudenosaunee eventually tried to return home, but

others never did, remembering there were no food stores and no homes. The invading army had eaten well and could only have survived to conduct such complete destruction by eating the Indians' own corn and vegetable reserves to the last scraps. The Indian refugees went, then, to find welcome among the Seneca community along Buffalo Creek to the south, and some crossed the Niagara and went north to Canada. Word was that the Mohawk leader Joseph Brant might be given enough land by the British to make homes for many, from any nation. There was talk of a single territory composed of all Haudenosaunee nations. But the confederacy was divided. Two nations, the Tuscarora and the Oneida, had chosen to ally with the rebels. Brant, allied with the British, had attacked the Oneida. This history made it difficult to imagine all living together in one place. And when Washington finally won, the confederacy faced a new reality. Their old ally was confined to the north, and the new nation to the east was making plans.

In the spring of 1789, the United States was set to begin its life under the Constitution. Self-evidently, the Indians were the first Americans, were allies or enemies at the borders of the nation, and continued to live within the thirteen states. The Constitution barely mentioned them—only once, in passing—as if they were not there at all. Yet the new government was very aware of their presence.

Relations with the Indians took up a significant portion of policy and diplomacy for the American nation's first leaders. The annals of the first Congresses cite Native American issues rather frequently, and for some periods, relations with them form much of the business at hand. For example, even while full ratification of the Constitution was very much in doubt, the Continental Congress enacted the 1787 Northwest Ordinance for territorial governance. The plan explicitly outlined a policy of peace toward Native people: "The utmost good faith shall always be observed towards the Indians; their lands and property shall never be taken from them without their consent; and, in their property, rights, and liberty, they shall never be invaded or disturbed, unless in just and lawful wars authorized by Congress." Ominously, though, the Northwest Ordinance also made very specific plans for how settlement would be encouraged and organized in the heartland of the territory that Indians still largely occupied. It also alluded to plans to be implemented only when the "Indian titles shall have been extinguished."

Once the Constitution was adopted, the first American government set out to make peace with Native American nations and to avoid costly wars. At the same time, it negotiated for Native nations to sell or cede lands in exchange for promises of assistance and eventual incorporation into the American republic. Peace and treaties opened the door for the new nation to spread rapidly into what had been Indian territory. For the Native nations, peace was also the most desired state. But they knew all too well that giving up land would only further diminish the territory in which their people could freely hunt and farm.

In January 1789 President Washington and Henry Knox, the secretary of war, directed Arthur St. Clair to Fort Harmar, in the Ohio country. He went to try to secure both cessions of land and peace, signing treaties there with the nations of the entire Old Northwest: the Potawatomi, the Sauk, the Delaware, the Wyandot, and the Ottawa, as well as the Six Nations.

By late in the spring of 1789, a runner arriving to Mary's welcome hearth to get a meal and share the news before heading off to the council houses in the east would indeed bring grave news. The nations in the west had been defeated in the Ohio Valley and in many areas of long security in the Old Northwest. Despite the treaties,

conflict had continued, more war was expected, and the reverbera-
tions would make the entire frontier, even Mary's now-peaceful valley, unstable and potentially unsafe.

Just five years later, though, a remarkable thing happened. The
Americans reached out to make peace with the Haudenosaunee
directly—and alone—and even offered to come to their homeland to
assure it. President Washington sent a tested representative, Timothy
Pickering, who took the better part of a week to carefully make a
new treaty in the heart of Seneca country at Canandaigua in 1794.
Pickering made many offers to ensure the Seneca and their five
brother nations would enjoy a lasting peace. It included a guarantee
that their land in the western part of New York was theirs to keep forever, or sell if they saw fit—the same land the Americans previously
claimed they had won in war. The treaty included the Genesee River
valley.

In 1797 Farmer's Brother, the Seneca chief, sold much of the
Genesee River valley. But he asked that Mary Jemison be given formal
title to her farm and its surrounding lands—for she was recognized
as being responsible for a large set of relations. Called the Gardeau
Reservation, the area amounted to over 17,000 acres. Though she lost
her second Seneca husband, Hiokatoo, in 1811, Mary continued to
live in the Genesee River valley and guide her children, seeing the
unending stream of settlers now fairly filling the wooded acres across
the river with cabins and farms. She came to be widely known, in
fact, as the White Woman of the Valley. Though she moved back to
the shores of Lake Erie just prior to her death in 1833, and still spoke
very little English, she eventually told her entire life story; and oddly
enough for the troubles she had with Americans, her narrative has
been read by many generations of them. The site of her cabin can be
visited today in Letchworth State Park. The only image of Mary is a
statue that was created many years after her death, but it does stand

where Mary would have looked out across the river gorge to the east, awaiting the unknown.

Mary's descendants still live today within miles of her cabin at Gardeau. Her great-great-grandson Peter Jemison directs the Seneca Art and Culture Center near Victor, New York, called Ganondagan, "Town of Peace," where there is a replica of a Haudenosaunee long-house from the seventeenth century and information about modern Seneca people and their lives. Their survival is due to their resilience and cultural cohesiveness first and foremost, but also because they steadfastly held to their traditional lands through the nineteenth century, which saw the arrival of increasing numbers of settlers who had no desire to keep the earnest agreements made in 1794 by Washington and his representatives on their behalf. One threat after another imperiled the Seneca, such as the coming of the Erie Canal in the 1820s, and later in that century, the nationwide attempt to remove all Native people to the west. Yet they fought each threat, and even as late as the 1950s, the Seneca had to go all the way to the Supreme Court to protest a federal dam-building project that would have flooded much of their land in western New York and force one traditional community to relocate. They lost much of their remaining land through such unceasing encroachments, but still retain their cultural and traditional lives on every part of their original home-land. Though Sullivan's army sought to erase the Haudenosaunee, they live on today; through Mary's words, we can begin to learn their side of the history of the age of revolutions.

CONCI

N O one has a right to compel me to be happy in the peculiar way in which he may think of the well-being of other men; but everyone is entitled to seek his own happiness in the way that seems to him best, if it does not infringe the liberty of others.

—*IMMANUEL KANT,* Principles of Politics, *1793. The German philosopher championed the ideals of the American and French revolutions, asserting the independence of the individual in the face of authority. Yet, perhaps ironically, Kant's principles of politics exclude a right to rebel.*

W OMEN ought to have representatives, instead of being arbitrarily governed without having any direct share allowed them in the deliberations of government.

—*MARY WOLLSTONECRAFT,* A Vindication of the Rights of Woman: With Strictures on Political and Moral Subjects, *1792. The English radical feminist challenged the long-standing notion that women were subordinate to men and demanded that women be treated as equal citizens, with equal legal, social, and political rights.*

USIONS

WHAT is the origin of that excessive inequality which concentrates all the wealth of the country in a few hands? Is it not bad laws, bad government, and the vices of a corrupt society?

—*MAXIMILIEN DE ROBESPIERRE, 1791, in a*
major speech linking civic rights with social justice

AFTER all, what makes any event important, unless by its observation we become better and wiser, and learn "to do justly, to love mercy, and to walk humbly before God"?

—*OLAUDAH EQUIANO,* The Interesting Narrative
of the Life of Olaudah Equiano, *1789*

CHALLENGING TIME

DR. JAMES HUTTON,
THE FATHER OF GEOLOGY

SALLY M. WALKER

DEEP THINKERS are as curious as the proverbial cat. Seventeenth-century thinkers grappled with a big question: How old is the earth? Genesis, the first book in the Bible's Old Testament, states that God created the earth in six days. Later, in the Bible's New Testament, 2 Peter 3:8 mentions "that one day is with the Lord as a thousand years, and a thousand years as one day." Using this logic, the earth would be six thousand years old (six days, each one thousand years long).

In the 1650s, biblical scholar Archbishop James Ussher went a step further. He combined information from biblical genealogies with the known chronologies of several non-Christian civilizations and declared that God created the earth on October 23, 4004 BC, at midday. Most Christians agreed the earth's age was about six thousand years. To believe otherwise would have been sacrilegious.

Some eighteenth-century people weren't convinced. By 1789 information contained in a science paper published the previous year had spread outward from Scotland. And the earth theory it proposed outraged many people.

The rumblings had begun in 1785, when Dr. James Hutton spoke to members of the Royal Society of Edinburgh, in Scotland. The society's members, who included Hutton, were a group of men who regularly met to discuss topics such as economics, poetry, science, history, and philosophy. Hutton was a deist, a person who believes in a particular version of a creator God. He believed that God created the earth. That God had wisely designed earth's processes—for example, those that formed land and oceans. After doing so, God did not remain actively involved in how those processes functioned. The theory that Hutton proposed in 1785 did not question how earth was created, but it disagreed with long-standing beliefs about the earth's age. He informed the society's members that his examination of England's and Scotland's soils and rocks convinced him that earth was vastly older than six thousand years. He concluded his presentation stating that his observations could "find no vestige of a beginning—no prospect of an end" when he tried to consider earth's age. Although there are no written accounts of how the audience responded to Hutton's theory, some listeners probably thought Hutton's radical conclusion—which differed from biblical scripture—was blasphemous.

James Hutton was born in Edinburgh, in 1726. His father, William, was a merchant and respected town official who died when Hutton was two years old. Afterward, Hutton's mother, Sarah, raised him and his sisters on her own. She realized that her son's future success depended on a good education. Like many boys whose parents could afford it, Hutton was probably tutored privately at home when he was very young. When he was ten years old, he enrolled in the Royal High School of Edinburgh, where he studied Latin, Greek, and mathematics, the subjects that boys typically studied during the eighteenth century. After he entered the University of Edinburgh, he attended a lecture that included information about chemistry. How chemical substances interacted with one another fascinated him. Hutton was hooked. At that time, chemistry was not a major course of study—knowledge of the subject had not yet developed to the level where it was regarded as a separate science. Determined to learn more, he read about the subject on his own. Even after graduating from the university, he continued to conduct chemical experiments, often neglecting the duties he'd been assigned at his job in a solicitor's law office to do so.

Hutton attended medical schools in Scotland, France, and the Netherlands, where he received a medical degree. One reason he chose to study medicine was that it included chemistry classes. He became interested in chemical experiments with minerals, the materials that are the building blocks of rock.

When he returned to Scotland, he decided not to practice medicine. Instead, he and a friend conducted chemical experiments on soot, a black substance produced by partially burned coal. Their experiment produced a rare mineral called sal ammoniac. This substance was used in manufacturing processes such as dyeing and cleaning metal. It was also often included as an ingredient in medicinal elixirs. The profits they made from producing and selling sal ammoniac provided Hutton with a lifelong income, which freed him to devote his full attention to a newfound interest, agriculture.

Hutton farmed for nearly twenty years, first in England, and later in Scotland on farm property left to him by his father. He noticed that grains of soil—their color and texture—varied from place to place and that many seemed to be tiny fragments of rock. He wondered how they related to larger rocks nearby. His mind overflowed with questions about the earth's surface.

In 1753 Hutton began searching the countryside for answers. Riding a horse, he spent days traveling from one place to another. To relieve a long journey's boredom, he often dismounted and studied the minerals and rock formations. Hutton climbed ridges and slid into gullies, peering with "anxious curiosity into every pit, or ditch, or bed of a river that fell in his way." In a letter to a friend, he lamented that the rear end of a person who hunted stones should be pitied. Sliding down rough hillsides and sitting on sharp-edged outcrops tore his clothes. More than four times in forty days, Hutton visited a tailor so he could have the seat of his trousers mended!

On his journeys Hutton saw massive rock formations made of sandstone. Some formations had distinct layers. The sandstone layers alternated and varied in color. Some were a reddish color; others were gray. In some places the layers lay horizontally, like the stacked layers of a cake. In other areas they were bent, folded, and even tipped vertically. They looked as though a great force had lifted and pushed them. Hutton wondered what kind of earth processes could do this. In 1768 he moved back to Edinburgh and devoted himself full-time to understanding the earth.

Scientists rely on observation to help them learn about the natural world. So it isn't surprising that Hutton believed that research and observation were the best ways to solve earth's puzzling past. His quest for knowledge about earth's history led to new journeys that crisscrossed Scotland. He closely observed mountains and the rock material that formed them. He collected an enormous quantity of rocks, which he called Bibles written "by God[']s own finger," and packed them into large barrels that he shipped to Edinburgh for further study.

He realized that over time the actions of wind and water eroded and broke apart rock material, relentlessly making the fragments smaller and smaller, until they became the tiny mineral grains found in soil. Wind sweeps soil from one place and deposits it in another. Flowing rivers carry sediments and rocks toward the ocean. He marveled that earth's processes were "so wonderful a curiosity." Hutton recognized that some changes—for example, a cliff's collapse—occurred swiftly. Others, like the rounded edges of a boulder or a rock that currents had rolled many miles along a riverbed, occurred slowly. But Hutton could tell from the kind of rocks that he found, and the places where he found them, that these things had, in fact, happened.

The wider his travels, the more rock specimens he collected. Eventually, he accumulated so many rocks that a visitor to his home reported that Hutton's study was "so full of fossils [rock and mineral samples] and chemical apparatus of various kinds that there is scarcely room to sit down." Hutton's thorough examination of rock formations and of specimens in his laboratory caused him to rethink the earth's age.

At the time Hutton began his travels, most scientists (the terms "geology" and "geologist" were not in popular usage until the last quarter of the eighteenth century) viewed the earth's formation very differently than we do in the twenty-first century. They believed that a global ocean once covered the newly created earth's surface. Some believed that land had already formed beneath the water and only appeared as the ocean evaporated. Others believed that land appeared gradually as the ocean evaporated and chemicals that had been dissolved by ocean water combined and crystallized to form minerals, which in turn formed rock. Both theories stated that earth's oldest rocks were found on mountaintops, the areas first exposed as the global ocean evaporated. Younger rocks were found at sea level. All of these scientists believed that the process of creating land occurred only one time. All other changes on the earth's surface, they assumed, occurred as the result of catastrophes, such as Noah's flood in the Bible. This dovetailed perfectly with the belief that earth was six thousand years old.

Hutton's years of investigation led him to a very different conclusion. He theorized that the creation of land was not a onetime event, but rather an endless cycle, like planets orbiting the sun or blood circulating throughout a body. His theory proposed that earth's land, water, and air interacted with one another in a vast cycle of processes that enabled earth to sustain itself. On land, everyone could see that rainwater, rivers, crashing ocean waves, and wind eroded the earth's surface. Hutton noted, "The heights of our land are thus leveled with the shores; our fertile plains are formed from the ruins of the mountains." People could see another part of the cycle along coastlines, where ocean waves pulled eroded sediments and rock fragments seaward. Hutton further stated, "We are certain that all the coasts of the present continents are wasted by the sea and constantly wearing away upon the whole, but this operation is so extremely slow that we cannot find a measure of the quantity in order to form an estimate [of how long it takes]."

Yet Hutton's theory did not end at the coastline. It extended into areas that people couldn't see—the deepest parts of the ocean and beneath the earth's surface. He believed that a wise God would not create a flawed system. New land would have to be created to offset the natural destruction of land. If it weren't, the earth would eventually run out of erodible land. He suspected that new land formed in parts of the cycle hidden from human eyes. The big question was how.

Again Hutton looked for answers by observing rocks. Some of the rock formations he examined contained seashells and fishes. They had fused with sediment grains and formed sandstone. He had no idea how long ago these fossilized sea creatures may have lived. But their presence proved something important. Even though Hutton found the layers as a mountainside, they had once been a sea-floor. The sandstones and their contents were evidence of an older world and a sea that had existed in another time. But how had they become rock?

On beach walks, Hutton would have found loose shells from sea creatures that had recently died. Many were similar to the fossilized shells in the rocks he had collected. It seemed reasonable to con-clude that the shells and sand that formed his rock samples had once been loose like the shells and sand that surrounded his feet. One of Hutton's good friends was a man named Dr. Joseph Black. He loved chemistry as much as Hutton did. Hutton learned something very important from Black: that intense pressure generates heat. Enough heat to fuse shells, rock fragments, and mineral grains. With this knowledge, Hutton envisioned the loose shells he saw being slowly carried out to sea. As time passed, accumulating horizontal layers of sediments and more shells would bury them on the seafloor. Being the first materials deposited, the loose shells he had seen would be the bottom (and oldest) layer. Hutton was certain that sometime in the future the pressure of the deep layers would cause the shells and sand grains he saw to fuse and form new rock. Still, recognizing that pressure could fuse materials did not explain what turned a sea-floor into a mountain. Hutton was convinced this important step was part of the cycle in which earth repaired itself and created new land.

During his many travels, Hutton also noticed another rock, called granite, which is often found high on mountains. This led early sci-entists—those who thought that mountaintops were the first land to appear as the global ocean evaporated—to label granite as the oldest kind of rock on earth.

Based on what he saw, Hutton disagreed. He found massive

veins of granite that in some places had squeezed into the layers of sandstone. In others, it had strong enough force to push completely through the sandstone and up to the surface. In both instances, the granite had to be younger than the sandstone and in a fluid, probably molten, state. (While sandstone is formed as one layer presses down on another—sedimentation—granite is formed in the intense heat of lava or magma and is called an igneous rock.) Further, the moving molten rock forced the sandstone out of its way. Very high heat and pressure can make a solid rock, such as buried sandstone, bend or fold. In places where conditions are cooler and under less pressure, the same rock would crack apart. As the molten rock cooled, it crystallized as granite. This process, like the layers produced by the fusion of sediments, also created new land. Yet almost without pause, its destruction would begin as air and water acted on it.

Hutton was certain that the earth processes that had formed the rock formations in England and Scotland operated similarly throughout the world. If people looked on any continent, they would find additional evidence that the land there was continuously destroyed and replenished, with a new version of itself replacing older ones. What had become very apparent to Hutton was that the transformation took time, more time than human history could measure. It was a cycle that seemingly had no beginning or end.

In 1785, when Hutton presented his theory to his colleagues at the Royal Society, some members flat out disagreed. Others grumbled skeptically. A few thought about it with open minds. However, all of them agreed: Hutton would have to find more evidence if he wanted them to believe it.

Hutton resumed his travels, finding rocky bits of evidence here and there. But he was looking for a massive rock formation that so clearly showed what he was talking about that it couldn't be ignored.

Months, then one year . . . two . . . slipped past. In 1788 the Royal Society of Edinburgh published the presentation that Hutton had read three years earlier as a scientific paper. It was titled "Theory of the Earth." News of his theory started to spread. The pressure was on to find the perfect rock formation.

One day in early June 1788, Hutton took advantage of "exceeding favourable weather" and arranged a boat trip that would depart from Dunglass, a town on Scotland's eastern coast, about thirty-five miles from Edinburgh. Two friends, minister and scientist John Playfair and geologist Sir James Hall, joined him on the adventure. Their friend's theory about the earth intrigued them, and they were excited to help him find proof.

As the boat sailed southeast along the coast, calm seas permitted the captain to "keep close to the foot of the rocks which line the shore." They journeyed toward a headland called Siccar Point. For countless years, waves crashed its coastline, scrubbing soil off the land and battering the bare rock after it had been exposed. The water's relentless onslaught wore some slopes smooth. Their force cracked and crumbled other parts of Siccar Point. Slabs of rock tumbled into the sea, creating a 200-foot-high perpendicular cliff. Layers of red and gray sandstone were perfectly exposed in both areas. Playfair noted that Hutton was "highly pleased with [the] appearances that set in so clear a light the different formations of the parts [layers] which compose the exterior crust of the earth." Siccar Point exhibited the exact proof Hutton had been seeking!

The boat landed and the three friends climbed the sloped rocks. They walked on the surface of exposed gray sandstone. They immediately noticed that the gray layer had been uplifted and tilted vertically. But in other areas, the gray sandstone was not exposed. Slanted layers of red sandstone still overlay it. The men looked closely at the areas where the red and gray sandstones touched. The jagged top of the gray sandstone proved that it had eroded before the layers of red sandstone had accumulated.

What Siccar Point showed and the scientists saw was the effect of time. The gray layers took time to accumulate. It took time for them to tip vertically and erode. It took more time for the layers of red sandstone to accumulate and be shifted from the horizontal. Trying to imagine, to comprehend, the amount of time needed to produce the whole sandstone rock formation awed Playfair, who wrote, "The mind seems to grow giddy by looking so far into the abyss of time." Equally amazed, James Hall sketched a drawing of the rock formation so he could share what they'd seen with others.

In 1789 Hutton and his friends continued to share their information with other scientists. Although they may not have realized it, 1788 and 1789 were revolutionary years in the emerging field of study called geology. Acceptance of a new theory takes time. Many of Hutton's colleagues still objected to Hutton's theory on religious grounds, clinging to biblical scholars' estimate that earth was six thousand years old. Some scientists disagreed with Hutton's thoughts about how heat affected rock that was buried beneath the surface. They could only imagine intense heat being caused by a burning flame. They knew a fire couldn't continuously burn inside the earth, a place that lacked oxygen. They couldn't grasp that a different kind of heat was inside the earth.

Hutton didn't give up. He continued his studies. In 1795 he published two volumes titled *Theory of the Earth, with Proofs and Illustrations*, in which he further discussed how people could discover information about past processes by observing present-day environments that were similar and noticing what processes were acting there.

Unfortunately, Hutton died in 1797. Defending his theory from further attack was left to his friends John Playfair and James Hall. Playfair collected and examined more rocks and wrote about them. He presented a talk at the Royal Society about Hutton and further clarified Hutton's theory. Hall experimented on rocks. His experiments disproved claims made by some of Hutton's detractors.

Within decades of 1789, other scientists based their own new theories on Hutton's ideas. Geologist Charles Lyell, born in Scotland the year Hutton died, further investigated Hutton's claims about earth's cyclic pattern of destruction and replenishment. He arrived at the conclusion, simply stated, that the present is the key to the past. Lyell shared his work with his good friend Charles Darwin. Although Darwin is most famously known for his theory of evolution and natural selection, he was first interested in geology. He realized that Hutton's and Lyell's ideas about how time could change earth's appearance might also be applied to living organisms.

Since the eighteenth century, geologists and other scientists have learned a lot about certain chemical elements and how long it takes the atoms of those elements to decay after a rock has formed. (Uranium, discovered in 1789 by Martin Heinrich Klaproth, is one of them.) They have invented instruments that can analyze a sample of a rock and measure how much certain atoms have decayed. Geologists have dated the sandstones at Siccar Point with these instruments. The older gray sandstone layers formed about 435 million years ago. After they formed, there was a gap of about 65 million years before the red sandstone layers were deposited. John Playfair described James Hutton as a man who had "a little more spirit and liveliness" than most other people. It is easy to imagine that Hutton would have been delighted to learn that the sandstones were so ancient.

James Hutton challenged time and people's conceptions about

the earth's age at a period when the quest for scientific knowledge was flourishing. Time has proven him correct. Hutton has rightfully earned the title of the Father of Geology. The sandstone layers at Siccar Point are still as vivid as they were when Hutton saw them, and Siccar Point is often called the birthplace of modern geology. Every year scores of interested people trek to Siccar Point to examine its compelling geology. Given Hutton's lively spirit, this would probably delight him too.

MUTINY ON THE *BOUNTY*

BREADFRUIT, FLOGGING, IMPOSSIBLE NAVIGATION, AND REVOLUTIONARY IDEAS— THERE OUGHT TO BE A MUSICAL

STEVE SHEINKIN

WILLIAM BLIGH, captain of the British Royal Navy's HMS *Bounty*, was shoved from his sleep by rough hands. Grumbling "What's the matter?" he opened his eyes to a shocking sight.

Four crewmen stood in the tiny, windowless cabin, glaring down at the captain with swords drawn, muskets aimed.

"Murder!" Bligh roared. "Murder!"

One of the intruders, a young officer named Fletcher Christian, ripped Bligh from bed by his nightshirt. The men pulled the captain's arms behind his back, bound his wrists with rope, and dragged him up to the main deck.

The sea was calm and the sky far to the east was just beginning to lighten. It was the morning of April 28, 1789.

Several sailors danced around the imprisoned captain, taunting him with bayonet blades, cursing him, laughing at the sight of this imperious man in nothing but a flimsy garment that barely reached his thighs. Other crewmen, Bligh noticed, were busy lowering one of the ship's rickety lifeboats down to the water. Why? To send him drifting to his death? Bligh turned to Christian, demanding answers.

"Hold your tongue, Sir," Christian shot back, his eyes flashing, his long black hair flowing in the breeze. "Hold your tongue, or you are dead this instant!"

That's how it began, the famous mutiny on the *Bounty*. It's a truly epic tale of adventure and treachery, romance and revenge, survival against all odds and mysterious disappearance. It's the inspiration for many movies and entire shelves of books. I couldn't possibly tell you this story in one brief chapter.

So here goes.

First of all, the fact that the mutiny occurred in 1789 was no coincidence. It was just six years since the end of the American Revolution. King George had lost his American colonies, and with them a reliable supply of food for the colonies that the British really cared about— their Caribbean islands. The sugar plantations on these islands, particularly Jamaica, were more profitable to Britain than those ungrateful Americans had ever been. British plantation owners began looking for a new source of food for the enslaved men, women, and children from Africa who were forced to work on the farms.

The British scientist Sir Joseph Banks had a suggestion. In his travels around the world, Banks had been intrigued by the potential of the breadfruit trees he'd seen on the Pacific island of Tahiti. A member of the fig family, breadfruit trees produce soccer-ball-sized fruits rich in nutrients and vitamins. Banks's idea was that a British crew should sail to Tahiti, gather saplings, bring them to the Caribbean islands, and plant the trees there.

Free food—King George liked the sound of that. The Royal Navy selected the *Bounty* for the mission, giving command to thirty-three-year-old William Bligh. Bligh had started as a captain's servant at age seven and joined the navy at sixteen. He was a respected officer and an expert navigator. At a time when commanders were virtual dictators, with the power to whip sailors for any minor infraction, Bligh was known for being "very passionate"—short-tempered, in other words, but not cruel.

Fletcher Christian, twenty-three, hired on as master's mate. The son of landowners, Christian could have afforded to stay in school; his older brother was a successful lawyer. He chose the sea instead. Christian was five foot nine (a bit taller than average for the time) with an athletic build. He had served with Bligh twice before. He looked up to the older man as a mentor.

The *Bounty*, with a crew of forty-six, sailed from Britain in December 1787.

Setting out for the southern tip of South America, the ship was battered back by storms and had to turn east instead and sail around the southern edge of Africa. The zigzag journey covered 28,000 miles (it's 24,901 miles around the entire globe at the equator) and took ten months.

The crew worked exhausting shifts and slept in cramped spaces with no privacy. They froze in the far south and boiled in the tropics, surviving on wormy biscuits, rotting fruit, slowly spoiling salted meat, and fetid water. Bligh drove his men hard and cursed them ferociously, but, true to his reputation, he resorted to the lash less often than many commanders. Bligh did have one sailor whipped for what he described as "insolence and contempt," and there was one death from disease, likely due to the fact that the ship's surgeon was, in the captain's bitter words, "in bed all the time intoxicated."

But by the standards of the day, it was a successful voyage. There was no hint of the trouble to come.

The *Bounty* dropped anchor in Tahiti's breathtaking Matavai Bay on October 26, 1788. Sailors from cloudy Britain gazed in awe at the turquoise water and lush green mountains, the white beaches lined with palm trees.

Bligh met the rulers of this region of the island, including a giant man named Tynah and his wife, Iddeah, the island's wrestling champion. In years to come, Tahitians would have cause to curse the arrival of European sailors, who brought diseases and guns to the island. For now, though, the leaders gladly agreed to trade breadfruit trees for iron nails and tools.

The *Bounty* men were in Tahiti for five months. Some collected breadfruit plants and others did routine maintenance on the ship, but there was less work than when they were at sea. The sailors spent free time on the island. They made friends; many formed relationships with women. They loved the warm climate and bountiful fresh food, the dances and sporting contests. They weren't being bossed around twenty-four hours a day. In short, they enjoyed a quality of life far beyond what young men without wealth or connections could ever expect in Great Britain.

This, in retrospect, may help explain the coming calamity.

Bligh, all the while, was a man obsessed. He was there to do a job, a mission that could make or break his future in the navy. The sight of his men enjoying themselves—going soft, in his view—irritated him more each day. Floggings become common, and the reasons flimsier. Bligh noted in his log that he gave Robert Lamb, the ship's butcher, twelve lashes for "suffering his cleaver to be stolen."

It was during this time that Bligh began clashing with Fletcher Christian. In early January 1789, three *Bounty* sailors deserted in a small boat with dreams of growing old in Tahiti. Bligh tracked the men down, flogged them—and blamed Christian, claiming Christian knew of the men's plans and had done nothing to stop them. Christian denied the charge. This became a pattern. "Whatever fault was found," a crew member would later testify, "Mr. Christian was sure to bear the brunt." Though not directly punished by Bligh, Christian was deeply hurt by such relentless criticism from a man he so admired.

Some of the sailors looked on with growing dread as the ship's botanist began moving potted breadfruit plants aboard the *Bounty*. For those of the crew who had no families at home, no chance of finding better-paying or less physically punishing jobs as they got older, what exactly did they have to look forward to?

The *Bounty* set sail for the Caribbean on April 4, 1789.

"Thus far," Bligh noted in his log, "I have accomplished the Object of my Voyage."

The ship was a floating garden. More than a thousand potted plants competed for the limited space on the *Bounty*'s decks and cabins. All that mattered to Bligh was to get those plants to the West Indies.

The captain's blow-ups, especially at Christian, grew more frequent. At a stop for fresh water at the Friendly Islands (now Tonga), Bligh lashed out at Christian for backing away from a confrontation with the island's inhabitants, calling Christian "a damned cowardly rascal" in front of the crew.

This was more than mere criticism—duels were fought over less. Christian sulked, his honor wounded.

All agree that the point of no return came on the morning of April 27. It was a warm day. The South Pacific sea was calm. Strolling the deck, Bligh glanced at the coconuts that the crew had gathered in Tahiti and piled between cannons. He turned to the ship's master, John Fryer.

"Mr. Fryer, don't you think that those coconuts are shrunk since last night?"

Fryer didn't think so.

Bligh insisted that coconuts had been "taken away" and vowed to find the culprits.

"Mr. Young—how many nuts did you buy?"

Edward Young, a midshipman, took a guess.

"And how many did you eat?"

Young took a guess, but it was absurd; no one was counting each coconut.

Bligh questioned all the officers, finally turning to Christian.

"How many nuts did you buy?"

"I do not know, Sir," said Christian, "but I hope you don't think me so mean as to be guilty of stealing yours."

"Yes, you damned hound, I do!" Bligh exploded. "You must have stolen them from me, or you could give a better account of them."

Turning on the others, he continued ranting. "You scoundrels, you are all thieves alike, and combine with the men to rob me. I suppose you'll steal my yams next, but I'll sweat you for it, you rascals! I'll make half of you jump overboard before we get through Endeavor Straits!"

The captain stomped below to his cabin.

The officers remained on deck, stunned and offended. Christian was devastated. Some recalled seeing tears on his cheeks.

Bligh, incredibly—cluelessly—invited Christian to dine with him in his cabin that evening. That was typical Bligh. Once the tantrum passed, he forgot all about it.

Christian refused the invitation and spent much of the night on deck in what would later be described as a highly agitated state. He would no longer serve under Bligh. His initial idea was to build a raft and paddle to the nearest island. But at some point before dawn, as he gathered supplies and talked quietly with trusted crewmates, he decided to seize command of the ship. All told, Christian recruited at least eight sailors to join his mutiny.

Claiming he needed a musket to shoot a shark, Christian asked Joseph Coleman, the armorer, for the keys to the ship's chest of weapons.

There really was a shark. Several men on deck, unaware of Christian's plan, leaned over the rail, watching the huge fish glide alongside the ship.

"What's the matter?" came a startled voice from below.

And then: "Murder! Murder!"

And this brings us back to where we began—the moment of history's most famous mutiny, the stunning scene of Captain Bligh, in his nightshirt, hands bound behind his back, being tossed onto the deck by Christian and his armed accomplices.

Several officers tried to talk Christian down from this rash action—the one and only punishment for mutiny was death by hanging. They urged him to think of the men not involved in the mutiny. How were they supposed to get home?

"Tis too late!" Christian roared back. "I have been in hell for this fortnight past and am determined to bear it no longer."

He ordered a lifeboat hoisted over the side, planning to send off Bligh and a few of his lackeys.

Bligh pleaded for another chance. "Consider, Mr. Christian, I have a wife and four children in England, and you have danced my children on your knee."

"You should have thought of them before," snapped Christian, "and not behaved so much like a villain."

The lifeboat was lowered to the water and supplies handed down. To Christian's surprise, most of the crew wanted no part of staying on the *Bounty* with mutineers. Nineteen men crowded into the ship's launch, a twenty-three-foot boat, and many more—we'll never know exactly how many—wanted to join. But the launch was already dangerously overloaded.

Bligh's men rowed slowly away, looking back at the *Bounty* as the mutineers sent a steady stream of breadfruit plants splashing into the sea.

We've seen Bligh at his worst—now we see his best.

He had twenty-eight gallons of water, a few hunks of salt pork, 150 pounds of bread. He had a pocket watch, a compass, and a quadrant—a tool used to calculate latitude by measuring the angles to stars. He had his memory of maps of the world's continents and oceans. Bligh leveled with the men. Their one chance to get home was to reach the port of Kupang on the island of Timor (now part of Indonesia), from where they could board a ship to Europe.

Timor, Bligh estimated, was four thousand miles away.

Storms battered the little boat for three straight weeks, and the men lived in soaked clothes that began falling apart. They bailed furiously to keep from sinking, tossing out water all day and through nights so dark the men couldn't see each other between bursts of lightning. They took turns curling up on the boat bottom and awoke too stiff to move. They lived on one ounce of bread and one-quarter of a pint of water per day.

When the seas finally calmed, the sun beat down and the weakened, weary men began to die of thirst. Day after day, Bligh kept the launch on course, urging his men never to lose heart. When they caught a pigeon-sized seabird by hand, Bligh cut the bird into tiny parts, saving the blood for the sailors nearest to death.

On June 13, forty-six days after the mutiny, the men spotted the island of Timor. They stumbled onto shore with tears of joy flowing from sunken eyes. The people of Kupang looked on in horror. Bligh understood why. "Our bodies were nothing but skin and bones, our limbs were full of sores, and we were clothed in rags."

William Bligh's 4,000-mile open boat voyage is one of the great survival stories of all time. Greeted as a hero when he returned to Britain in early 1790, Bligh quickly published a best-selling narrative of his adventures. A new play called *The Pirates; or, The Calamities of Capt. Bligh* hit the London stage.

The Royal Navy, meanwhile, wanted very much to know what had happened to their ship—and why.

Bligh had had plenty of time to think about this, and the theory he formed actually ties in nicely with the larger theme of the human struggle for rights in 1789. The mutiny, Bligh argued, was not sparked by shipboard insults or missing coconuts, but by the fact that Christian and his fellow mutineers could not resist the lure of a better life. "What a temptation it is to such wretches," Bligh explained, "when they find it in their power, however illegally it can be got at, to fix themselves in the midst of plenty in the finest island in the world where they need not labour."

Was it that simple? Most of the mutineers had earned their living aboard ships since the age of ten or younger. They had little hope for advancement and no chance to be financially secure as they grew older and less able to work. Did the mutineers simply want to live a freer, easier life in Tahiti? Does that make them, in their own way, revolutionaries?

Or were they just criminals looking to lounge on the beach?

Can the truth be somewhere in between?

Like any good story from history, this one evades easy answers—

we don't really know what the sailors were thinking. And what about Christian? He *did* have a future to look forward to back in Britain. Was his pride really *that* shattered by a few insults? Was he determined to return to the woman he'd left behind in Tahiti? Was he standing up for those less able to act?

It's tempting to see Christian as one of history's great loose-cannon bad boys, throwing it all away to strike one blow against tyranny. But, again, we don't know what he was thinking in the hours and minutes before the mutiny.

Fletcher Christian was never caught. It was not from a lack of trying.

On the morning of March 23, 1791, an eighteen-year-old *Bounty* midshipman named Peter Heywood stepped out of the cottage he shared with his wife in Tahiti, looked out at the harbor, and was surprised—but hardly shocked—to see the Royal Navy's HMS *Pandora*.

He knew the British would come looking sooner or later.

Peter had been sixteen at the time of the mutiny. He hadn't helped Christian but had hesitated in joining Bligh in the lifeboat. Now, nearly two years later, he lived happily in Tahiti and was fluent in the language. When he saw the British ship, he figured he had nothing to fear; he wasn't a mutineer, after all. He swam out to greet the British sailors.

The *Pandora*'s captain, Edward Edwards, seized the teenager, declared him a "piratical villain," and slapped him into irons.

Edwards rounded up fourteen of the *Bounty*'s crew in Tahiti. Most claimed to have played no part in the mutiny, but Edwards's mission was to get the men back to Britain and let a naval court sort the guilty from the innocent. Peter Heywood and the others were locked inside a wooden shack on the *Pandora*'s deck—Pandora's Box, the prisoners acidly dubbed it. They lay naked on rough planks in leg irons and handcuffs, coated with sweat and maggots. Peter could hear his wife calling through the wall, begging to see him, to at least be permitted to say goodbye. Captain Edwards refused.

Fletcher Christian was not found in Tahiti. The prisoners explained to Edwards that Christian and eight of the known mutineers had sailed away eighteen months before in search of a remote island hideaway. The *Pandora* set out to find them. And now the story starts taking twists that would make movie audiences roll their eyes. It's just too much.

After three miserable months of fruitless searching, the *Pandora* crashed into the Great Barrier Reef and cracked open. Peter Heywood made it out of Pandora's Box, but four of the prisoners drowned. The surviving prisoners and crew—including two young officers who'd been with Bligh on his open boat voyage—climbed into lifeboats and set out on a similarly hellish trip to Timor. Peter and the other *Bounty* prisoners spent the entire time chained to the bottom of the lifeboats. If anyone dared object, or so much as groan, Captain Edwards growled: "You piratical dog, what better treatment do you expect?"

The court-martial of the *Bounty* prisoners opened in September 1792. The other major story in the news was the increasingly bloody French Revolution, which terrified the ruling classes of England.

It was not a good time to be seen as a rebel.

A panel of naval officers in dark blue coats presided over the trial in the great cabin of a ship in Portsmouth harbor. The space was crowded with prisoners and witnesses, family members and curious spectators. Bligh was not there—he'd been sent back to Tahiti to attempt the breadfruit mission again.

The *Bounty* sailors described very different versions of the mutiny, with different combinations of people under arms alongside Christian. When asked by the court why he hesitated to join Bligh in the launch, Peter Heywood cited his "extreme youth and inexperience."

Four of the sailors were acquitted. The others, including Peter, were convicted. Vice Admiral Lord Hood read the order for "each of them to suffer Death by being hanged by the Neck."

Peter spent the next month in prison, racing to finish a dictionary of the Tahitian language before his execution. But there was still hope—mostly thanks to Peter's older sister. Hester Heywood, "Nessy" to the family, worked the case tirelessly, firing off letters to influential family friends. It worked. Peter (along with one other convicted man, James Morrison) was personally pardoned by King George. On the drizzly morning of October 29, with crowds watching from land and from ships in the harbor, the other four *Bounty* prisoners were hanged to death on the deck of the HMS *Brunswick*.

Bligh's second mission to Tahiti was a success. Nearly seven hundred breadfruit saplings were planted in Jamaica. The trees thrived and bore fruit—and the people hated it. They fed the tasteless mush to the pigs.

Breadfruit eventually caught on as creative cooks found ways to use it, and it's an important part of Jamaican cuisine today.

Where was Fletcher Christian? That was the *Bounty*'s great unsolved mystery.

Christian's vanishing act inspired its share of wacky theories. Several people even claimed to have spotted the infamous outlaw lurking on dark lanes in the Lake District of northern England, near the home of a woman who'd once rejected him.

More concrete evidence was finally found in 1808, when an American ship, *Topaz*, stopped at a small South Pacific island that had been badly misplaced on existing maps. Captain Mayhew

Folger's best guess was that it was Pitcairn Island. The place looked uninhabited, with waves crashing on rocky cliffs and no natural harbor.

Folger was surprised to see three teenagers paddling toward him in canoes. And he was downright shocked when one of them addressed him in English, introducing himself as Thursday October Christian.

Folger didn't make the connection right away.

Then the boy asked, "Did you ever know Captain Bligh?"

And that's when Folger realized he'd solved the mystery. Rowing ashore with Fletcher Christian's son, the captain met women, children, and one elderly man. The man, John Adams, confessed to having been one of the *Bounty* mutineers. Christian and the mutineers, he explained, had sailed to Pitcairn Island with twenty Tahitians, fourteen of them women. They'd settled on the island, but the English men's cruel and racist treatment of the Tahitians led to war. All the men died, save for Adams.

Today about fifty people, descendants of Tahitian women and the mutineers, still live on Pitcairn Island.

Over time, as the *Bounty* saga was told and retold in books, plays, and eventually movies, the characters took on predictable roles. Bligh became the snarling villain, Christian the romantic hero. Maybe that image of Christian standing on the deck, sword raised and hair flowing, is just too good to resist.

There's a lot more to the story, of course. That's the great thing— there always is.

AUTHOR NOTES

AMY ALZNAUER—"PI, VEGA, AND THE BATTLE AT BELGRADE"

When I began researching this essay, I was already a lover of pi, already amazed by that deceptively simple constant at the heart of the circle yet seemingly everywhere. Pi appears not just in geometry, but in many of the most important and far-reaching ideas in mathematics: the Heisenberg uncertainty principle, formulas describing planetary and periodic motion, Einstein's theory of general relativity, and all sorts of famous integrals and infinite series. Like I said in the essay, it's enough to make you think mathematics lies at the heart of everything.

So, I was quite familiar with pi, but not with Jurij Vega. When I first looked him up, he seemed like nothing more than an entry in a long list of digits-of-pi discoverers. But eventually, as I dug into the holdings of Slovenian libraries, the life of Vega and the world surrounding him began to open up.

Vega was no longer just a name, but an orphan, a seeker, a restless intellectual who changed his name to reflect his ambition, an activist and a warrior, a husband and an innovator. He became a person I could imagine standing in the rain on a battlefield or under a single star at night. He became for me the distant brother of Archimedes and a quintessential Enlightenment figure.

The principle is similar for the number and the man. By homing in on the simple ratio of a circle's circumference to its diameter, we discover pi, which then becomes one of the keys to unlocking far-flung secrets of the universe. And by homing in on a single name in a long list of names, we discover not just the full life of a human being, but one of the keys to understanding a whole era. So yes, the details matter. The poet William Blake, who was born just three years after Vega, beautifully described the power of details, which can allow us to glimpse "a world in a grain of sand" and "eternity in an hour."

My work has won the Annie Dillard Award for Creative Nonfiction, the Christopher Award, and the SCBWI-Illinois Laura Crawford Memorial Mentorship. My books for children include *The Boy Who Dreamed of Infinity: A Tale of the Genius Ramanujan*; *Flying Paintings: The Zhou Brothers: A Story of Revolution and Art*; and *The Strange Birds of Flannery O'Connor*. I hold an MFA in creative writing from the University of Pittsburgh, teach calculus and number theory classes at Northwestern University, serve as the managing editor for the SCBWI-Illinois newsletter *Prairie Wind*, and am the writer in residence at St. Gregory the Great, where I have a little office in a big building with a bad internet connection, so I can actually get some work done (in theory).

MARC ARONSON—"THE CHOICE: PARIS, 1789"

When I worked on my doctorate in American history, some of my most enjoyable reading centered on the period of the American Revolution. Just as I entered graduate school, historians drew ever more heavily on the work of anthropologists, trying to see a time and a place through the eyes of the people who lived then and there. For example, in his brilliant *The Transformation of Virginia*, Rhys Isaac begins his book by comparing how the Virginia countryside would look from the vantage of a squire riding on a horse versus an enslaved person walking. They would literally be experiencing different landscapes in the same location. The other major discussion and debate about that period had to do with the idea of "republicanism" (not related to the modern political party). This was an effort to understand what the very words used by the founders meant to them, and thus how they envisioned the new nation. Researching this chapter gave me the chance to return to those books and to the worlds of the eighteenth century.

There are a great many books about Thomas Jefferson's time in Paris reflecting different interests and points of views held by the historians who wrote them. A crucial divide comes on the question of how to see Jefferson's relationship with Sally Hemings. During their lifetimes, Madison Hemings and other members of the family gave interviews, wrote accounts, and gave clear statements of their family connection to Jefferson. However, the dominant view of the most respected historians, such as Dumas Malone, who wrote a multivolume biography of Jefferson, was to discount these stories. They could not reconcile the man they thought him to be and a man beginning a lifetime relationship with an enslaved teenager, his wife's half-sister. That began to change in the 1970s, when professor Fawn Brodie wrote a psychological biography of Jefferson that assumed he did have a relationship with Hemings, and then more actively from 1998 on, when DNA tests showed that a male Jefferson was the ancestor of a branch of the Hemings family. The test could not prove that it was Thomas, but he was the male Jefferson who was in physical proximity to Sally Hemings when the children were likely conceived. Based on her own extensive research and the DNA evidence, Annette Gordon-Reed in her 2008 book *The Hemingses of Monticello* treated the records left by the Hemings family as likely to be accurate personal recollections—which is how I have used them here. To understand how Jefferson reconciled his positions on enslavement, I relied on a book Gordon-Reed coauthored with Peter S. Onuf, another highly respected Jefferson scholar, *"Most Blessed of the Patriarchs": Thomas Jefferson and the Empire of the Imagination.*

The idea that Jefferson saw himself as a biblical patriarch comes from the latter book. The Virginia gentry did often see themselves as both virile—strong, manly providers who in effect created abundance for all those under their protection—and virtuous: public citizens who lived by an honor code and were duty bound to help shape politics and society. It is easy to see how this view flattered the men, marginalized women, and cast enslaved people as dependent inferiors. Yet there is much to be learned from trying to understand, rather than merely anachronistically condemning, those beliefs and self-images.

I knew of Annette Gordon-Reed's *The Hemingses of Monticello* from when it was published to extraordinary reviews. Working on this essay gave me the chance to read it and the book she wrote with Peter Onuf and to explore the literature around Jefferson, Hemings, and 1789.

My next sole-authored book will be a history of Manhattan in four streets and a square.

SUSAN CAMPBELL BARTOLETTI—"THE QUEEN'S CHEMISE: ÉLISABETH VIGÉE LE BRUN, PORTRAITIST OF MARIE ANTOINETTE"

Many years ago, I found myself drawn to the work of Élisabeth Vigée Le Brun, whose painting I first saw on display in the National Gallery of Art in Washington, DC, and then again when I toured the palace of Versailles in France. I knew that I wanted to write about Élisabeth and the ill-fated queen Marie Antoinette someday.

To research this essay, I brushed up on my French (long over-due!) and focused my study on Élisabeth's relationship with Marie Antoinette and four of her renderings of the queen. The dramatic structure of these paintings formed a natural narrative arc against the backdrop of the Enlightenment period and the French Revolution.

I give hearty thanks to author-illustrator Ashley Wolff and to Dorothy Kelly, an independent scholar whose doctoral research focused on female artists in Europe, for our discussions about art and about the paintings I chose for this essay.

My latest nonfiction book for young readers is *How Women Won the Vote: Alice Paul, Lucy Burns, and Their Big Idea* with archival images and full-color illustrations by Ziyue Chen.

SUMMER EDWARD—"THE WESLEYANS IN THE WEST INDIES"

Growing up in Trinidad and Tobago in the 1990s, I was raised Catholic and attended an all-girls Catholic high school. The chapel at my high school and the Catholic Church just down the hill where students attended mass were filled with statues of Jesus, the Virgin Mary, and the biblical saints. The statues did not have brown skin like the majority of Trinidad and Tobago's population, myself included. I wondered about these things. Was Christianity created by white people? Were God and the angels white? How did so many people of color living on a Caribbean island end up wholeheartedly espousing a faith whose iconic imagery did not include people who looked like us or lived where we lived? The questions I had never seemed to end, and yet I felt like there were no adults I could turn to who would entertain my questions in a serious way. To my adolescent self, there seemed to be a huge silence around the racial aspects of religion in my island.

The order of nuns who lived in the convent next to my high school, and who gave us home economics lessons and religious instruction, had first arrived in Trinidad and Tobago in 1836 and had been founded by a white French nun named Anne-Marie Javouhey, known as the Liberator of the Slaves in the New World. Javouhey had grown up during the French Revolution, which began in 1789, and its discourse of egalitarianism profoundly influenced her life's work. I didn't know any of this when I was in high school. In those days in Trinidad, slavery was not taught until the fourth form (i.e., the ninth grade), so I was already fifteen years old when I was first privy to a formal discussion about colonization and slavery in the Caribbean; unfortunately, it was a very limited discussion that did not answer many of the questions I had.

In doing research for this essay, I wanted to gain an honest understanding of why eighteenth-century Methodist missionaries risked their lives to travel to the Caribbean and convert slaves who already had a strong African religious heritage. What were their real motivations? To answer this question, I read the journals and other writings of Methodist missionaries and leaders, including John Wesley and Dr. Thomas Coke, as well as official Methodist Church records from the eighteenth and early nineteenth centuries. *The Arminian Magazine*, founded by Wesley, was an especially valuable resource. I also read excerpts from disquisitions on the topic of slavery written by abolitionists who were Methodists.

A burning question I imagined every reader would have was, what did enslaved people think about the missionaries' attempts to Christianize them? I read relevant sections of the few known Caribbean slave narratives, including *The History of Mary Prince*; *The Interesting Narrative of the Life of Olaudah Equiano, or Gustavus Vassa, the African*; and *The Narrative of Archibald Monteith, a Jamaican Slave*. Lastly, I used whatever credible sources (books and web resources)

I could find on the history and development of the Methodist Church in the Caribbean. Other helpful texts and memoirs I read are listed in the bibliography.

It is important for young people today, particularly those growing up in post-colonial societies, to have a clear understanding of what was lost and what was gained in the long process of colonization and Christianization that continues even today. Looking back at my younger self, I desperately needed access to real, honest discussions about race, religion, and the crossroads where they meet in order to build a strong sense of self. If you can find people in your life who are willing to have these serious conversations with you, and if you begin at a young age to define your views on race and religion for yourself, you can gain wisdom, that much-needed guiding light on your path through the world.

For the past nine years, I've been the editor in chief of *Anansesem*, an online publication I founded devoted to publishing and covering English-language Caribbean children's and young adult literature. I've sat on judging and manuscript review panels for children's and youth writing competitions, including the Golden Baobab Prize for African children's literature, the Scholastic Art and Writing Awards, and the OpenIDEO Early Childhood Book Challenge. My writings on childhood literacy and multicultural children's literature have appeared in *The Horn Book*; *WOW Stories: Connections from the Classroom*; *sx salon*; *Literacy Daily* (the official blog of the International Literacy Association); *Charlotte Huck's Children's Literature: A Brief Guide*; the EBSCOhost NoveList readers' advisory database; and more. My writing for adult readers has appeared in two anthologies, *New Daughters of Africa* and *New Worlds, Old Ways: Speculative Tales from the Caribbean*, and in numerous literary journals.

I recently left my teaching job at the University of the West Indies and am now working as a readers' advisory specialist at EBSCOhost

NoveList while polishing my children's book manuscripts and teaching yoga classes. My first children's book, *Wygenia and the Wonder of the World Leaf*, will be published by HarperCollins UK in 2020. A dual citizen of the United States and Trinidad and Tobago, I divide my time between the two countries.

KAREN ENGELMANN—"THE CONTRADICTORY KING: GUSTAV III AND THE UNLIKELY BEGINNINGS OF CLASS EQUALITY IN SWEDEN"

Eighteenth-century Swedish history is not high on most reading lists. It wasn't on mine, not even during the nearly ten years I worked as an illustrator and art director in Malmö, Sweden. But the dramatic story of King Gustav III and the legacy of that period are woven into Swedish culture and permeate the capital city of Stockholm. Unbeknownst to me, the seed of a particular passion was planted. It bloomed several decades later when I wrote a novel set in the Gustavian period as my thesis project for a master of fine arts in creative writing. (This is the sort of quixotic—aka crazy—choice one makes as a beginner.)

I took it as a good omen that the college library had a copy of *The Life and Songs of Carl Michael Bellman* by Paul Britten Austin (1967). Bellman was a musician, poet, and notorious part of Stockholm society of that time, and this wonderful book provided entry to the colorful life of "The Town" and the court of Gustav III. I was hooked and ready to dive deep! The challenge was getting ahold of research material—most of which is in Swedish. Fortunately, my language skills proved adequate, and friends in Sweden generously provided me with books (and a twenty-five-pound Swedish dictionary). It was slow going at times, but the history was thrilling and mostly unknown to English-language readers. My novel—*The Stockholm Octavo*—was published in 2012 and translated into fourteen languages. It's fiction with a large dose of fantasy, but it's built on a firm foundation of facts that research provided.

The writing for *1789* required a closer look at the political situation of the day, and I relied on three sources in my collection: in Swedish, *Historien om Sverige: Gustavs Dagar* by Herman Lindqvist (1997) and *Gustaf III:s Stockholm* by Christopher O'Regan (2004), and in English, *Gustavus III and His Contemporaries, 1742–1792*, vol. 2, by Robert Nisbet Bain (1894). The reading and writing have inspired me to dig deep again. Maybe Queen Christina this time . . . I'll need to dust off that dictionary.

Joyce Hansen—"'All Men Are Created Equal': The Global Journey of Olaudah Equiano"

We've had a long relationship—Olaudah Equiano and I. Many years ago, I discovered his narrative in the collection *Great Slave Narratives*, edited by Arna Bontemps. I think I picked it up because I was intrigued by the title. I wasn't researching the subject of slavery. I read this book long before I'd written any of my historical fiction and nonfiction.

The book contained Olaudah's narrative along with two others. Once I began reading, I was pulled into his world and couldn't put it down. Olaudah tells the story of his short time as a free African child, the horrific events of his kidnapping, his experience on the slaver ship, and his forced entry into a new life. His story is so much more than what happened to him outwardly though. He also brings us into his inner life, revealing his soul, his humanity, and his deep spirituality—from which he drew his strength. He was able to look in the eyes of the man who owned him and say, "I am free; you cannot by law serve me so." What a powerful statement. He was already free in his own mind.

Many years after reading Olaudah's narrative, I was asked by one of my editors whether I had any ideas for a new book. I had already written several middle-grade novels and one work of historical fiction. I remembered Olaudah's story. Actually, I had never forgotten it.

I wrote my historical novel *The Captive* in the style of a slave narrative, using Olaudah's autobiography as the prototype. If you read Olaudah's narrative and my story, you would see instances where I was inspired by Olaudah—my character Kofi's frightening experience on the slaver, being forced into a boxing match with a young white boy for the entertainment of the sailors on the ship, the first time he sees snow, and his learning how to read and write were all inspired by Olaudah's narrative. My novel *The Captive* was published in 1994, and I did not read Olaudah's narrative again until I was asked to contribute a chapter for *1789*.

I reread the entire narrative for the third time in order to write "'All Men Are Created Equal.'" It was like visiting an old, inspirational friend. I am struck by how Olaudah still speaks to us in the twenty-first century.

When I read his words describing his concern about the victimization and sexual abuse of women and girls on the slave ships, I think of today's #MeToo movement. If Olaudah were still with us, he would've marched in solidarity with the girls and women speaking out against those same issues. When I read his poignant description of being separated from his sister, I think of the children today who are separated from families and loved ones for any number of reasons. He would have raised his voice in protest. And he shows us how we are all demeaned when we do not acknowledge one another's humanity. I am pleased to be able to introduce Olaudah to a new generation of readers.

Cynthia Levinson and Sanford Levinson—"Who Counted in America? The Beginning of an Endless Conversation"

Our chapter in *1789* is one of a number of pieces we've written together. The first and longest is our book *Fault Lines in the Constitution: The Framers, Their Fights, and the Flaws That Affect Us Today*.

As you can probably tell from the title, the book focuses on problems built into the foundations of our government that continue to reverberate. Some of the issues we address—especially the Electoral College and the Senate—relate directly to the questions we raise in *1789*: Who counts? And does everyone count equally?

In 1787 James Madison called the arrangement that gives two senators to every state, no matter the size of its population, an "evil." Today this situation is even worse. Most Americans squeeze into only nine states, which send a total of eighteen senators to Congress. That means that less than half the population lives in the remaining forty-one states and sends a whopping eighty-two senators to Washington, DC. If you live in California, your vote and the issues you care about—forest fires, say, or traffic jams—count less than those of people who live in Wyoming. Furthermore, since every state's Electoral College members equal the number of its representatives in the House plus its two senators, big states also count less than small states when choosing the president.

The endless conversation about who counts in America has been going on since at least 1787. It just takes different forms over time.

Our view that the Constitution is seriously flawed has already had an effect. A play called *What the Constitution Means to Me*, which ran on Broadway, ends with a spontaneous debate between the playwright, Heidi Schreck, and a high school student. Their topic is "Resolved: The Constitution should be abolished." While we probably would have used a less sensational word, like "replaced" instead of "abolished," the debate was inspired by our book. We even got to do a talkback after one of the performances!

We hope that you will continue to talk and read about problems with the Constitution, so that you are counted in, not out.

Cynthia's turn: Having spent thirteen years in all-female schools, I've long been concerned about the role and voices of women in our society. After working in education for many years, I now write nonfiction books for young readers about social justice, including racism (*We've Got a Job: The 1963 Birmingham Children's March*; *The Youngest Marcher: The Story of Audrey Faye Hendricks, a Young Civil Rights Activist*; and *A School for Problems: Myles Horton and the Highlander Folk School*), children in conflict zones (*Watch Out for Flying Kids: How Two Circuses, Two Countries, and Nine Kids Confront Conflict and Build Community*), and the labor movement (*Ben Shahn: The People's Painter*). Thanks to my research and writing, I've had the opportunity to walk with foot soldiers of the civil rights movement, fall off a tightwire and a rolling globe, stay with a family in an Arab village in the Galilee, and read letters housed in a condemned building surrounded by yellow police tape.

Sandy's turn: After graduating from Duke and getting a PhD in government from Harvard and then a law degree from Stanford, I briefly practiced law for the Children's Defense Fund and taught at Princeton. The first job led to an ongoing interest in the extent to which we treat young people as full-fledged citizens with the right to express their point of view. I also litigated a case defending the rights of mentally disabled people. I joined the University of Texas Law School faculty in 1980. I've been teaching and writing for more than forty-five years about how people are treated under the United States Constitution. Contrasts and similarities among the US and other national constitutions, including the French, as well as American state constitutions have been a central focus of my recent work, especially as revealed in the title of my book *Framed: America's 51 Constitutions and the Crisis of Governance*. (Cynthia is especially proud of the pun in the title. I'm pleased to remind readers that every state plus the District of Columbia and Puerto Rico has its own constitution.)

STEVE SHEINKIN—"MUTINY ON THE *BOUNTY*: BREADFRUIT, FLOGGING, IMPOSSIBLE NAVIGATION, AND REVOLUTIONARY IDEAS—THERE OUGHT TO BE A MUSICAL"

I didn't like history as a kid. At least, I didn't think I liked it. I thought history was where you memorize a bunch of names and dates and regurgitate them onto a test paper and then forget them.

But when I look back at the books I read over and over in those years, the list is filled with history. Train robberies, buried treasure, underdog sports stories, epic adventures. Some of it was nonfiction, and some, like the *Mutiny on the Bounty* trilogy by Charles Nordhoff and James Norman Hall, was historical fiction. Anyway, I obviously *did* like history—it just took me a while to realize it.

As an adult, and a proud history nerd, I casually collected books about the *Bounty* saga, picking up volumes at used bookstores here and there, always saying to myself, "Someday I'm going do something with this story." But other than a short comic I drew years ago in which I imagined me as a kid joining the *Bounty* crew, I haven't tried to write about this story until now. The good news is, when I took on the project, I was far ahead of where I usually am when I begin something new. I had a shelf of books ready to go. I'd read most of them. I'd taken notes on some favorite parts.

That's how I always begin a new nonfiction project—a stack of books and lots of notes. I started with a few well-researched narrative histories of the *Bounty* saga, including Caroline Alexander's *The Bounty* and Sam McKinney's *Bligh*. The great thing about books like these is that you get the big picture of the story, and, in the source notes, you get a list of places to find more information. I'm particularly on the lookout for primary sources. In the case of the *Bounty*, you've got Bligh's own account of the mutiny, accounts from other sailors, and even the transcript of the mutiny trial, in which many of the sailors had a chance to speak.

As I said in my chapter, there's more than enough story here for a whole young adult nonfiction book on the *Bounty*. I don't know if I'll ever write it—but I hope someone does!

TANYA LEE STONE—"'THE FISHWIVES MAKE THE RULES': THE OCTOBER DAYS OF THE FRENCH REVOLUTION"

My feminist roots run deep. I owe some credit to memories I do not consciously remember, some of which happened long before I was born. Stories of female perseverance and strength hang like lush leaves in the foliage of my family tree. In the time span of my own life, I have had the good fortune to be given models to mirror in my grandmother, her sisters, and my personal pillar of strength through good times and bad, my big sister.

The path I seem to be pursuing in life is that of historian, teller of true stories. Perhaps the bit of my own history I have shared serves to explain why I am intent on filling in some of the many missing gaps—the lack of inclusion—in our history books. I find myself continually compelled to tell the true stories of women whose ideals and actions shape our world. Nothing thrills me more than discovering fierce female narratives begging to be more widely known.

When given the opportunity to learn something I don't know, I feel grateful. That was the dominating emotion I had when I was asked to contribute to this anthology and shown the list of topics that were being considered for the year 1789. The women's march for bread on Versailles caught my immediate attention. I jumped at the chance—as I tend to do when seeing there is yet another incredible story about women I know nothing about—to immerse myself in the research and get to know this story well enough to tell it to readers like you.

Searching through the stacks of the UVM library in Burlington, Vermont, I was able to find enough chapters and snippets to begin to shape my sense of what happened in those October days. This research was helped immeasurably by a new book by a contemporary historian who began her research for her undergraduate thesis and continued to follow the threads of that story long after graduation. I believe Katie Jarvis has published one of the only scholarly books inspired by this episode in history. Please see the bibliography for sources you may wish to use to follow the threads that most intrigue you.

Some of my other books include *Almost Astronauts: 13 Women Who Dared to Dream*; *Courage Has No Color: The True Story of the Triple Nickles*; *Who Says Women Can't Be Doctors?*; and *Girl Rising: Changing the World One Girl at a Time*. Forthcoming titles include *Remembering*

Rosalind and *A Story of War, a Story of Peace*. You can find more of my book titles, as well as contributions to anthologies, interviews, and articles, on my website.

I dedicate this story to my beloved niece, Sarah Alexis, a sixth-grade history teacher who was obsessed with Marie Antoinette.

CHRISTOPHER TURNER—"MARY JEMISON AND THE SENECA NATION: 1789"

Growing up in upstate New York, I first came to know of Mary's story the way many do today: through a visit to Letchworth State Park, the site of Mary's Gardeau cabin, where a statue of her commemorates her life and role as a transitional figure on the frontier between the time when the Haudenosaunee controlled the area and the arrival of the settlers who came to possess much of it. The park is a wonder of natural beauty with three stunning waterfalls, a dramatic, deep gorge, and of course the silent but stately Genesee River flowing to its end in Lake Ontario. Anyone can see why Mary took particular pride in the location. In addition to Mary's cabin site, some interpretive efforts are there as well to reward an inquisitive person: a Seneca longhouse from the early nineteenth century was moved there from a community that was relocated at that time. Some artifacts of Seneca life are found in a small, dusty museum just a bit off the beaten path. But this is not how most have come to know Mary's story—her life was made famous by a biography published in 1856, by James Seaver, who actually listened as Mary recounted her life to him. Scholars today classify her life story within a genre of literature unique to American literature called "captivity narratives" and consider why, across a surprising range of time periods, people were thrilled to read about the experiences of Euro-Americans who were taken captive amid conflicts with Native people in much of the east and lived among them for a time. It is worth noting that very few Europeans, once taken captive, were harmed, and some, like Mary, lived for long periods of time in their adopted community. Mary is hardly alone among women captives who elected to stay among the Native people who took them into their societies.

For myself, it would be some years before I pursued a specific interest in Haudenosaunee culture formally as a cultural historian, though they are the Native people of my home region, and I grew up among Cayuga descendants. But only after obtaining my degrees in American studies and applied anthropology and working closely with Native people of Maine, the Passamaquoddy and Penobscot, as well as the Potawatomi of Indiana, where I undertook doctoral studies at Purdue University, did I return to New York to become something of a public historian, teaching college history by day but also becoming very involved in advocacy roles to improve education about the history of the Native people of the region. I was active in an organization that commemorates the Treaty of Canandaigua, the 1794 agreement by which the United States returned much land to the Seneca and promised a future relationship of peace with and independence from the United States, as referenced in the chapter. I was instrumental in a campaign to rectify the land loss of the Cayuga Nation through an organization called Strengthening Haudenosaunee-American Relations through Education (SHARE). And I have spent much time over the years with Mary's descendant G. Peter Jemison as he developed the Seneca Art and Culture Center at Ganondagan. I attend the yearly festival of contemporary Haudenosaunee music, dance, and lifeways that is open to the public on the last weekend of July. From Peter and many, many other Haudenosaunee cultural knowledge bearers, I am extremely grateful to have learned much—indeed, profound aspects of Haudenosaunee life and history far beyond

just the importance and details of Mary's life. For interested readers, I certainly recommend the biography of Mary Jemison called
A Narrative of the Life of Mrs. Mary Jemison, edited by June Namias,
which includes her excellent discussion of its role within American
literature. Also recommended is a general history of the Seneca over
this period by Laurence M. Hauptman, *Coming Full Circle: The Seneca
Nation of Indians, 1848–1934*, and for an overview of Haudenosaunee
culture generally, see the *Encyclopedia of the Haudenosaunee (Iroquois
Confederacy)* by Bruce Elliot Johansen and Barbara Alice Mann.

SALLY M. WALKER—"CHALLENGING TIME: DR. JAMES HUTTON, THE FATHER OF GEOLOGY"

When I was a little girl, I liked playing in the dirt, making mud pies,
and looking for interesting rocks. My interest in soil and rocks continued in college. I first heard about James Hutton in Geology 101,
a class that I took in my freshman year. Everything I learned that
semester, particularly the "stuff" about layers of rock, which is called
stratigraphy, fascinated me. Enough that geology (and archaeology) became my major. My future husband majored in geology too,
and many of our dates were field trips to look at rock formations or
to collect fossils. For me, reading a rock formation is like solving a
puzzle. It's fun to mentally untangle a complex series of layers that
have been folded, fractured, and eroded (by the processes that
Hutton wrote about) and determine the order in which they formed,
from youngest to oldest.

One of the many things I admire about James Hutton was his
commitment to presenting a revolutionary theory about the earth's
age. It isn't easy to stand firm when championing a new idea, especially when it contradicts generally accepted beliefs. I also applaud

his tenacity in seeking the evidence that substantiated his theory and using it to convince others. Hutton's quirky sense of humor gave me a chuckle or two. Having spent many hours kneeling in the soil and/or sliding down rock formations, I can personally attest to his statement that fieldwork is tough on clothing.

On visits to England and Wales, I've seen rock formations that Hutton saw. I haven't visited Siccar Point. Yet. But it's high on my bucket list. In the meantime, I sometimes pretend I am Hutton by watching a video about Siccar Point that was made by the British Geological Survey. You can find it at https://www.youtube.com/watch?v=JCEDCcHcpYE.

Warning: It will make you want to visit Scotland and maybe even study geology!

I've been an author of nonfiction books for young readers for a number of years and have written more than fifty books. My favorite subjects are those that combine history, mystery, and science. The research for my book *Written in Bone: Buried Lives of Jamestown and Colonial Maryland* was a fascinating adventure, since I was able to use my knowledge of geology and archaeology as I excavated eighteenth-century burials. Writing my book *Earth Verse: Haiku from the Ground Up* gave me the chance to play with language and geology. Many times people have told me that I have "rocks in my head." It makes me laugh, because they're right!

SOURCE NOTES

Exhilaration

p. 6: "Oh! pleasant exercise . . . very heaven": Wordsworth, *The Prelude: The Four Texts (1789, 1799, 1805, 1850)* (New York: Penguin, 1995), 441.

p. 6: "But Europe . . . born again": Wordsworth, *The Prelude*, 227.

p. 7: "We see the solemn . . . of man": quoted in J. C. D. Clark, *Thomas Paine: Britain, America, and France in the Age of Enlightenment and Revolution* (Oxford University Press, 2018), 244.

p. 7: "I have lived to see . . . irresistible voice": Richard Price, *A Discourse on the Love of Our Country*, in *The Works of Dr. Richard Price with Memoirs of His Life*, ed. William Morgan (London, 1816), 49.

"'The Fishwives Make the Rules': The October Days of the French Revolution" by Tanya Lee Stone

p. 11: "I present us . . . Nobility & the Clergy": Jarvis, *Politics*, 37.

p. 11: "want all the profit . . . spit on us down below": ibid., 38.

p. 13: *"les poissardes font la loi"*: Garrioch, 241.

pp. 13–14: "Go ahead, behave yourselves . . ." and "We're going to Versailles; . . . end of a sword": Dawson, 59.

p. 14: "found the King's Guards . . . what they wanted of the king": "Women Testify."

p. 14: "fell on her knees . . . fainted at his feet": Jarvis, *Politics*, 17.

p. 15: "Do what you are asked . . . we have our arms raised": Melzer and Rabine, 84.

p. 16: "The only thing left for me to do was to seize the movement": Shapiro, 91.

p. 16: "The miserable creatures were . . . in horrible disorder": Jarvis, "Allez, Marchez Braves Citoyennes," 56–57.

p. 17: "I jumped from my bed and ran to the window!" and "I really thought it was the last instant of my life": Dawson, 52.

p. 18: *"Le Roi à Paris! Le Roi à Paris!"*: Hibbert, 102.

p. 18: "Messieurs, I gave my word . . . worthy to be your leader": Jarvis, "Allez, Marchez Braves Citoyennes," 70.

pp. 18–19: "Long live the Body Guards!"; "What! Alone on the balcony . . . made against me?"; "Yes, Madame, go ahead"; "Long live the queen!": ibid., 71.

p. 19: "At one o'clock": "View from the Top."

"The Contradictory King: Gustav III and the Unlikely Beginnings of Class Equality in Sweden" by Karen Engelmann

p. 21: King Gustav III of Sweden watched . . . and took action to consolidate his power: Lindqvist, 184, 188, 439, 444–448. A contradiction from the start, Gustav championed King George at the beginning of the American Revolution. Over time, Gustav came to admire the revolutionaries' fervor. In a letter, the king presciently wrote, "Perhaps we find ourselves now in the American century." However, Gustav saw the French Revolution as a threat to the world order. His support for the French monarchy was lifelong and unwavering, and he took direct action to rescue the royal family.

p. 21: His adversaries . . . a coup and revolution in one: Lindqvist, 88, 396; Bain, 77. The Swedish constitution of 1720 had effectively created an aristocracy, but Gustav revised it after his coronation in 1772, returning government to a form closer to that of Gustav II from 1634—a limited monarchy. The new constitution maintained a parliament but restored far-reaching powers to the king and essentially negated all laws instituted since 1680. Gustav further consolidated his hold during the meeting of Parliament in 1789. Legislation enacted at this parliament changed Sweden from a limited monarchy to a near despotic one.

p. 21: The First Estate held a seventeen-year grudge against the king: Lindqvist, 88; Bain 77. The nobility's hold on power was broken.

p. 22: There were whispers and plots about deposing Gustav . . . then replacing him with his younger brother Duke Karl: Lindqvist, 465.

p. 22: Karl was all in favor of this . . . having himself anointed king in 1784 when Gustav was traveling in Italy: ibid., 135, 256.

p. 22: They were a miserable couple: ibid., 24, 154–159. Danish princess Sofia Magdalena was engaged to Gustav at age five, married by proxy at nineteen, then came shortly after to Stockholm. She was shy and religious, and neither Gustav nor the rambunctious court life suited her. Their sex life was the subject of much malicious gossip, including the rumor that their son had been fathered by the king's stable master, Adolph Fredric Munck.

p. 22: He felt they were the highest and best of humanity: ibid., 38–39, 396.

p. 23: The king praised the commoners' valor and patriotism . . . but he did not like their company: Bain, 52; Lindqvist, 24, 396.

p. 24: Gustav was counting on their support in the upcoming Riksdag of 1789: Bain, 47–48.

p. 24: The empress believed it just a matter of time . . . cowardly character: The empress saw Gustav as "a scoundrel and a poltroon, unworthy of the place he occupies" (ibid., 45).

p. 25: But Gustav's love for Sweden trumped all other passions: Gustav traveled with his troops and engaged directly in battle. In preparing for war with Russia, he was heard to say, "If I am driven to defend my realm, I'll show the world that I'm man enough to defend it well" (ibid., 15). Modern war historian Gunnar Arteus believes Gustav III had the potential to be a great warrior king (Lindqvist, 428).

p. 26: Gustav told his advisory council, the Senate, that Sweden must take immediate action: Bain, 15–16.

pp. 27–28: The burghers and peasants accused the nobles of cowardice and treachery . . . describing them as traitors and paid spies of Russia: ibid., 49–50.

p. 29: Gustav knew the Act of Unity and Security would inspire opposition or possibly outright revolt, even with his loyal commoners: ibid., 47–48. Keenly aware of the nobility's now-boiling resentment toward his constitution, Gustav understood that all four estates might see the act as the instigation of an absolute monarchy.

p. 29: even women (with restrictions), would have the ability to purchase land owned by the state and aristocracy: As in most of late eighteenth-century Europe, Swedish women lived in a patriarchy. They could not vote or hold office, few were educated, and their main role was childbearing. They could own property— through inheritance, dowry, gifts, or, in rare instances, purchase—but said property was controlled by either husband, father, or appointed male guardian. This information was gleaned from Åsa Karlsson Sjögren, *Kvinnors Rätt I Stormaktidens Gävle* [The judicial status of women in seventeenth-century Gävle] (Uppsala: Swedish Science Press, 1998).

p. 30: Unlike their French counterparts—aristocratic women who supported reform—Swedish women of position and power worked furiously *against* any changes to the status quo rather than for them: Lindqvist, 391, 434–435, 460. By 1789, the noblewomen of Sweden (including his sister and sister-in-law) firmly opposed Gustav. Only a handful of close female friends remained by his side until the end.

p. 30: Historians offer several theories: Bain, 66; Lindqvist 396, 643. Gustav remained a monarchist to the end, but his early exposure to the Enlightenment writers, his admiration for the American revolutionaries, and his careful study of the British two-chamber parliament, along with the unfolding drama in France, may have influenced his decision to allow for such significant social reform.

"Pi, Vega, and the Battle at Belgrade" by Amy Alznauer

p. 35: "immense masses of stone that came down with incredible noise and violence" and "knock down those upon whom they fell in heaps": Plutarch, 254.

p. 35: "Do not disturb my circles": This is the translation of Archimedes's legendary last line, *"Nōlī turbāre circulōs meōs!"* The only version that dates to antiquity comes from Valerius Maximus in a slightly different form, translated as "I ask you not to disturb that sand." Valerius Maximus, *Memorable Doings and Sayings*, vol. 2, books 6–9, ed. and trans. D. R. Shackleton Bailey (Cambridge, MA: Loeb Classical Library, Harvard University Press, 2000), book 8.7, ext. 7.

p. 38: "telescope" the series: Sandifer, 250.

p. 38: if you took a circle with diameter . . .: ibid., 251.

p. 38: "The reign of mathematics is over" and "Tastes have changed": Henry, 315.

p. 38: Lagrange felt that "perfection of details" seemed . . . "easier to exploit": ibid., 311. When he writes "perfection of details," Lagrange is actually quoting Jean Baptiste Joseph Delambre to convey his own thoughts. The rest is his.

p. 38: "mere amusements in geometry" and "as sordid and ignoble the whole trade of engineering": Plutarch, 250.

pp. 38–39: "Give me a place to stand on and I will move the earth": Thomas, 35.

p. 39: "theoretical concerns with practical applications": Perlman and Razpet, 407.

p. 39: A recent commentator claimed . . . as a calculator: Sandifer, 254.

Abomination

p. 42: "The French had shown . . . their manufactures": Edmund Burke, *The Works of the Right Honourable Edmund Burke*, vol. 3 (London: Henry G. Bohn, 1855), 271.

p. 42: "made and recorded a sort of institute . . . perhaps, many such": ibid., 275.

p. 42: "irrational, unprincipled . . . tyrannical democracy": ibid., 273.

p. 43: *"The rights of man . . . rights of babies!"*: Hannah More, *The Complete Works of Hannah More* (New York: Harper & Brothers, 1935), 338.

"The Queen's Chemise: Élisabeth Vigée Le Brun, Portraitist of Marie Antoinette" by Susan Campbell Bartoletti

p. 45: "You will be a painter . . . ever was one": Vigée Lebrun, 6.

p. 46: Élisabeth detested her stepfather: ibid., 12.

p. 47: "to make virtue attractive . . . chisel": Diderot, 78; see also Fried, 80.

p. 47: As a female artist . . . wasn't permitted to study the nude human figure: May, 11.

p. 50: "To anyone who has not seen the queen . . . dissipated": Vigée Lebrun, 57.

p. 50: Élisabeth found a long and oval face: ibid., 28.

p. 50: "I have never seen one . . . in any other woman": ibid., 28.

p. 51: Above on the gilded mantel . . . even if she did not: Zaleski.

p. 51: "Your large portrait pleases me": Sheriff, 164.

p. 52: two *livres*: Higonnet, 156.

p. 52: "a remarkably stupid person": ibid., 156.

p. 53: In 1783 . . . viewed *The Straw Hat*, an oil painting rendered by Peter Paul Rubens in 1625: Vigée Lebrun, 38.

p. 53: Later Élisabeth noted: ibid., 38–39; May, 43.

p. 55: Soon vicious accusations circulated: May, 45–47.

p. 55: Swedish military attaché Count Axel Fersen: Covington; see also Zaleski.

p. 57: A French fashion magazine: Interested readers can view the engraving at https://collections.mfa.org/objects/352862.

p. 57: Wicked people: Vigée Lebrun, 29. "Wicked people" is also translated as "malignant folk."

p. 57: "With this revolution in dress came a revolution in good manners": Fauveau, 50.

p. 58: "All that I have heard tonight . . . turned upside down": Vigée Lebrun, 17. That night Vigée had dined with the philosophers Denis Diderot, Claude Adrien Helvétius, and Jean le Rond d'Alembert.

"The Choice: Paris, 1789" by Marc Aronson

p. 64: "she could not die happy . . . never marry again": Gordon-Reed, 145.

p. 65: "substitute for a wife": Gordon-Reed and Onuf, 127.

p. 67: "very handsome" . . . "down her back": Gordon-Reed, 271.

p. 67: Jefferson believed in his own dreams . . . labor in the fields: Gordon-Reed and Onuf, 124.

pp. 67–68: "No young girl . . . seen as an enemy": Gordon-Reed, 307.

p. 68: "From what we now see . . . may be looked for": Ferling, 181.

p. 69: "born free and remain free . . . that injures no one else": ibid., 161–162.

p. 69: "Have you forgotten . . . born free and equal": O'Brien, 286.

p. 70: "loose and rambling . . . sparkled from him": Ferling, 207.

p. 72: "It is charming to be loved by everybody": Gordon-Reed, 304.

p. 73: "is worse than death . . . never see them again": "From Thomas Jefferson to Maria Cosway."

p. 73: "Jefferson loved her dearly": Gordon-Reed, 372.

p. 73: "Everything in this world . . . see which preponderates": "From Thomas Jefferson to Maria Cosway."

p. 73: "she refused to return with him": Gordon-Reed, 326.

p. 74: "Why have you not married . . . own color": Gordon-Reed and Onuf, 128.

p. 75: "Any lady is able to tell . . . from the clouds": Gordon-Reed, 346.

"'All Men Are Created Equal': The Global Journey of Olaudah Equiano"
by Joyce Hansen

p. 76: "I was born in the year . . . nor of the sea": Bontemps, 5. The fertile valley he mentions was in the kingdom of Benin, in West Africa, and is today part of southeastern Nigeria.

p. 76: "runaway best seller": ibid., xiv. https://pages.shanti.virginia.edu/Marking _Up_Johnson/the-interesting-narrative-of-the-life-of-olaudah-equiano/

p. 77: "The first object . . . deck and fainted": ibid., 27–28.

pp. 77–78: "One day when all our people . . . mouth": ibid., 20–21.

p. 79: "I had been travelling . . . being together": ibid., 23–24.

p. 79: "I was now more miserable . . . riveted my heart": ibid., 24.

p. 80: In 1788, a year before . . . anti-slavery publications: Franklin, 48.

pp. 80–81: "I was soon put down . . . example": Bontemps, 28–31.

pp. 81–82: "I remember, in the vessel . . . slavery": ibid., 33.

p. 82: "I stayed in this island . . . for North America": ibid., 34.

p. 82: "I had seen . . . muzzle": ibid., 34.

p. 83: "While I was on board . . . ever since": ibid., 36.

pp. 83–84: "it was almost a constant practice . . . account": ibid., 73–74.

p. 84: "These overseers . . . uncomfortable state": ibid., 74–75.

p. 84: "I told him . . . serve me so": ibid., 63.

p. 85: "original free African state": ibid., 105.

p. 85: "is a respected forerunner . . . 1830s": Equiano, 339.

pp. 85–86: "principal instrument in bringing about the motion for a repeal of the Slave-Act": ibid., 332.

p. 86: "more use to the Cause than half the People in the country": ibid., 394.

p. 87: A scholar writing . . . narrative: ibid., xxix.

Inspiration

p. 88: "What penalty . . . must live": quoted in Peter McPhee, *Robespierre: A Revolutionary Life* (New Haven, CT: Yale University Press, 2012), 142.

p. 88: "Let us arm ourselves . . . or in courage": quoted in John A. Lynn II, "Essential Women, Necessary Wives, and Exemplary Soldiers: The Military Reality and Cultural Representation of Women's Military Participation (1600–1815)," in *A Companion to Women's Military History*, eds. Barton C. Hacker and Margaret Vining (Netherlands: Brill, 2012), 131.

p. 89: "But the rights of men . . . same rights": quoted in *Continental Philosophy in Feminist Perspective: Re-reading the Canon in German*, eds. Herta Nagl-Docekal and Cornelia Klinger (University Park, PA: Pennsylvania State University Press, 2000), 35–36.

"The Wesleyans in the West Indies" by Summer Edward

pp. 91–92: "When shall the Sun . . . wings": Wesley, *Works* (Harper), 141.

p. 92: only certain people have been "elected" by God: This theological belief in salvation only for God's chosen elect is known as the doctrine of predestination; Methodism's refutation of predestination is discussed in Wesley, "Predestination," 256.

p. 92: "I look upon all the world . . . salvation": Wesley, *Journal*, 138.

p. 93: "To stir up all parties . . . truth": Wesley, *Works* (Carlton & Porter), 716.

p. 94: "Delightful" "tranquil" "simple-hearted": Coke, *Extracts*, 121–123.

p. 94: By the middle of 1789: For numbers of Methodists in the West Indies in 1789, see Goveia, 291. The Methodist *Conference Minutes* reported a West Indian Methodist membership of 11,170 in 1799 and 12,057 in 1800, as quoted in Norris, 213.

p. 95: "The immense mass of heathenism . . . people": Duncan, 8.

p. 95: "The second evening . . . From their design": Coke, *History*, 415–416.

p. 96: "were frequently so hooted . . . them": Sergeant, 21.

p. 96: George Stanbury, enslaved: George Stanbury's plight is mentioned in Findlay and Holdsworth, 120.

p. 97: "servants, be obedient . . . masters": Eph. 6:5 (KJB).

p. 97: "a dangerous fanaticism . . . revolt": quoted in Watson, 103.

p. 97: Methodists were compelled: See Matthews, 82–87, for a discussion on how anti-slavery advocates exonerated missionaries from accusations of inciting slave revolts.

p. 98: "The poor slaves . . . hours": Coke, *Extracts*, 91.

pp. 98–99: "While we were at Date Hill . . . *must* go": Prince, 16.

p. 99: "Like some poor pris'ner . . . released": Equiano, 153.

p. 100: "hired himself from his owner . . . good": quoted in Findlay and Holdsworth, 97.

p. 100: Sophia Campbell . . . Mary Alley: These black and mulatto Methodist leaders are mentioned in ibid. and in Aymer, 52.

p. 100: Throughout the British West Indies: For more on segregated church seating in the British West Indies, see Beasley, 33–36.

p. 100: sexual exploitations: On the other hand, there are historical accounts of corrupt Christian church leaders committing acts of violence and abuse toward slaves. Finkelman, 531, mentions that English-born Presbyterian minister and abolitionist George Bourne publicly challenged the conduct of another Presbyterian minister who severely abused his female slave. See also Bourne, 105, for Bourne's condemnation of "girl-selling, pimping" preachers. Sinha, 172, notes that "Bourne reserved his special ire for the hypocrisy of religious leaders, especially the elders and ministers of his church, whose abuse of slaves he had witnessed."

p. 102: John Wesley said no: John Wesley and Charles Wesley, 3–12; Wesley, "Farther Thoughts," 95–97.

p. 102: And if so, to paraphrase: quoted in Misra, 38. Despite his moral stature in the history books, Gandhi was not perfect and a complex figure; he expressed intolerance toward black South Africans and "lower caste" Hindu Indians. However, his views changed over the course of his lifetime, reflecting his ethical evolution.

"Who Counted in America? The Beginning of an Endless Conversation" by Cynthia Levinson and Sanford Levinson

p. 105: "Massachusetts is our country" and "Virginia, Sir, is my country": quoted in Davidson et al., 196.

p. 105: "The principle of all sovereignty . . . nation": "Declaration of the Rights of Man—1789."

p. 106: "imbecility": *The Federalist Papers*.

p. 107: the people are "dupes": quoted in Beeman, 114.

p. 107: "the instances will be very rare . . . United States": quoted in Raphael, 162.

p. 110: "parchment barriers": *The Federalist Papers*.

p. 111: "The people are waiting . . . decisions are made": quoted in Bordewich, 93.

p. 111: "to indulge": quoted in Remini, 32.

p. 111: "a tub thrown out to a whale": quoted in ibid.

pp. 111–112: "It will be much better . . . too much": Debates in House of Representatives, August 17, 1789, 11: 1291–1292.

p. 112: "a frequent call . . . necessary": quoted in Remini, 33.

p. 112: "the most valuable amendment . . . state governments": Debates in House of Representatives, August 17, 1789, 11: 1291–1292.

p. 114: "a free white person . . . of good character": "An act to establish an uniform Rule of Naturalization."

p. 114: "Whoever . . . by cursing . . . jail": 191st Court of the Commonwealth of Massachusetts.

"Mary Jemison and the Seneca Nation: 1789" by Christopher Turner

p. 119: "if I should be so fortunate . . . could not endure": Seaver, p. 131.

p. 120: "The Covenant Chain": Jennings, 88–96.

p. 121: "cut off their settlements": Mann, 56.

p. 121: "effect the complete devastation": ibid., 56.

p. 121: "Our corn was good": Seaver, 69.

p. 122: Hanadagá:yas, or "Town Destroyer": Mann, p. x; for Washington's orders: ibid., 55–56, and for his original wording and context, see Sparks, ed., *The Writings of George Washington; Being His Correspondence, Addresses, Messages* [. . .], Volume 6.

p. 122: Yet the new government: Prucha, 50–54.

p. 122: The annals of the first Congresses: see, for example, *The Journals of the Continental Congress, 1774–1789*, vol. 34 (Washington, DC: Library of Congress, 1904–1937).

p. 123: "The utmost good faith . . . been extinguished": Prucha, 47.

p. 123: Once the Constitution was adopted . . . Indian Territory: Horsman, 61; Prucha, 50.

p. 123: For the Native nations . . . hunt and farm: Horsman, 59–61.

Conclusions

p. 126: "No one . . . liberty of others": Eamonn Butler, *Classical Liberalism: A Primer* (London Publishing Partnership, 2015), 118.

p. 126: "Women ought to . . . of government": Mary Wollstonecraft, *A Vindication of the Rights of Woman: With Strictures on Political and Moral Subjects* (London: T. Fisher Unwin, 1891), 220.

p. 127: "What is the origin . . . corrupt society": quoted in McPhee, 95.

p. 127: "After all, what makes . . . before God"?": Olaudah Equiano, *The Interesting Narrative of the Life of Olaudah Equiano, or Gustavus Vassa, the African, Written by Himself*, 1789.

"Challenging Time: Dr. James Hutton, the Father of Geology" by Sally M. Walker

p. 129: October 23, 4004 BC: For an in-depth discussion of how Ussher selected this date, see Gould, 12–21.

p. 130: "find no vestige . . . end": Hutton, "Theory of the Earth," 304.

p. 132: "anxious curiosity . . . in his way": Playfair, 44.

p. 132: More than four times in forty days: Jones, Torrens, and Robinson, 648.

p. 132: "by God[']s own finger": quoted in ibid., 649.

p. 133: "so wonderful a curiosity": quoted in ibid., 646.

p. 133: "so full of fossils . . . to sit down": quoted in Jones, 229.

p. 134: "The heights . . . of the mountains": Hutton, "Theory of the Earth," 215.

p. 134: "We are certain . . . an estimate." Hutton, "Theory of the Earth," 301.

p. 137: "exceeding favourable weather": Hutton, *Theory of the Earth: With Proofs and Illustrations*, 1: 454.

p. 137: "keep close . . . line the shore": Playfair, 71.

p. 137: "highly pleased . . . crust of the earth": ibid., 72.

p. 138: "The mind . . . abyss of time": ibid., 72.

p. 139: "a little more spirit and liveliness": ibid., 44.

"Mutiny on the *Bounty*: Breadfruit, Flogging, Impossible Navigation, and Revolutionary Ideas—There Ought to Be a Musical" by Steve Sheinkin

p. 141: "What's the matter?" and "Murder!": Alexander, 266.

p. 142: "Hold your tongue, Sir . . . this instant": Bligh, 118.

p. 143: "very passionate": Alexander, 58.

p. 144: "insolence and contempt": McKinney, 32.

p. 144: "in bed all the time intoxicated": McKinney, 51.

p. 144: "suffering his cleaver to be stolen": Alexander, 115.

p. 145: "Whatever fault was found . . . the brunt": Bligh and Christian, 135.

p. 145: "Thus far . . . my Voyage": Alexander, 124.

p. 146: "Mr. Fryer, don't you think . . . through Endeavor Straights!": The coconut scene is recounted in virtually every *Bounty* source, including John Barrow, 87–88; Alexander, 134–135; and McKinney, 76.

p. 147: "Tis too late! . . . no longer": McKinney, 82.

p. 147: "Consider, Mr. Christian . . . like a villain": Alexander, 140.

p. 149: "Our bodies . . . clothed in rags": Bligh, 169.

p. 149: "What a temptation it is . . . not labour": McKinney, 88.

p. 150: "piratical villain": ibid., 145.

p. 151: "You piratical dog . . . expect?": ibid., 154.

p. 152: "extreme youth and inexperience": Tagart, 105.

p. 152: "each of them to suffer Death . . . Neck": Alexander, 283.

p. 153: "Did you ever know Captain Bligh": ibid., 347.

BIBLIOGRAPHY

"'The Fishwives Make the Rules': The October Days of the French Revolution" by Tanya Lee Stone

Abray, Jane. "Feminism in the French Revolution." *American Historical Review* 80, no. 1 (February 1975): 43–62.

Dawson, Philip. *The French Revolution*. Englewood Cliffs, NJ: Prentice-Hall, 1967.

Garrioch, David. "The Everyday Lives of Parisian Women and the October Days of 1789." *Social History* 24, no. 3 (October 1999): 231–249.

Hibbert, Christopher. *The Days of the French Revolution*. New York: William Morrow, 1980.

Hufton, Olwen. "Women in Revolution 1789–1796." *Past & Present*, no. 53 (November 1971): 90–108.

Jarvis, Katie L. "Allez, Marchez Braves Citoyennes: A Study of the Popular Origins of, and the Political and Judicial Reactions to, the October Days of the French Revolution." BA thesis, Boston College, 2007.

———. *Politics in the Marketplace: Work, Gender, and Citizenship in Revolutionary France*. Oxford: Oxford University Press, 2019.

Melzer, Sara E., and Leslie W. Rabine. *Rebel Daughters: Women and the French Revolution*. Oxford: Oxford University Press, 1992.

Racz, Elizabeth. "The Women's Rights Movement in the French Revolution." *Science & Society* 16, no. 2 (Spring 1952): 151–174.

Shapiro, Barry M. *Revolutionary Justice in Paris, 1789–1790*. Cambridge: Cambridge University Press, 1993.

"Stanislas Maillard Describes the Women's March to Versailles (5 October 1789)." Liberté, Égalité, Fraternité: Exploring the French Revolution. Accessed October 3, 2019. http://chnm.gmu.edu/revolution/d/473.

Tackett, Timothy. *The Coming of the Terror in the French Revolution*. Cambridge, MA: Belknap Press of Harvard University Press, 2015.

"View from the Top: The October Days." Liberté, Égalité, Fraternité: Exploring the French Revolution. Accessed October 3, 2019. http://chnm.gmu.edu/revolution/d/305.

Vittonati, François. "July 4, 1789: 'A Revolt? No, a Revolution!'" *Sun-Sentinel*, July 14, 1989.

"Women Testify Concerning Their Participation in the October Days (1789)." Liberté, Égalité, Fraternité: Exploring the French Revolution. Accessed October 3, 2019. http://chnm.gmu.edu/revolution/d/474.

"The Contradictory King: Gustav III and the Unlikely Beginnings of Class Equality in Sweden" by Karen Engelmann

Bain, Robert Nisbet. *Gustavus III and His Contemporaries, 1742–1792*. Vol. 2. London: Kegan, Paul, Trench, Trübner & Co., 1894.

Lindqvist, Herman. *Historien om Sverige: Gustavs Dagar* [The history of Sweden: Gustavian days]. Stockholm: Norstedts Förlag, 1997.

O'Regan, Christopher. *Gustaf III:s Stockholm*. Stockholm: Bokförlaget Forum, 2004.

"Pi, Vega, and the Battle at Belgrade" by Amy Alznauer

Beckman, Petr. *A History of Pi*. New York: St. Martin's Press, 1976.

Gay, Peter. *The Enlightenment: The Rise of Modern Paganism*. New York: W. W. Norton, 1995.

Henry, Paul. "On Mathematics at the Time of the Enlightenment, and Related Topics." In *Skill, Technology and Enlightenment: On Practical Philosophy*, edited by Bo Göranzon, 311–326. London: Springer-Verlag, 1995.

Košir, Matevž. "Brother Vega, Freemason." In *Jurij Baron Vega in Njegov Čas: Zbornik Ob 250-Letnici Rojstva* [Baron Jurij Vega and his times: Celebrating 250 years], edited by Tomaž Pisanski et al., 177–204. Ljubljana: DMFA—založništvo, Arhiv Republike Slovenije, 2006.

Malleson, Col. G. B. *Loudon: A Sketch of the Military Life of Gideon Ernest, Freiherr Von Loudon, Sometime Generalissimo of the Austrian Forces*. London, 1884.

Maximus, Valerius. *Memorable Doings and Sayings*. Vol. 2, books 6–9. Edited and translated by D. R. Shackleton Bailey. Cambridge, MA: Loeb Classical Library, Harvard University Press, 2000.

O'Connor, J. J., and E. F. Robertson. "Georg Freiherr von Vega." January 2012. http://www-groups.dcs.st-and.ac.uk/history/Biographies/Vega.html.

Perlman, Mihael, and Marko Razpet. "Jurig Vega and Ballistics." In *Jurij Baron Vega in Njegov Čas: Zbornik Ob 250-Letnici Rojstva* [Baron Jurij Vega and his times: Celebrating 250 years], edited by Tomaž Pisanski et al., 395–408. Ljubljana: DMFA—založništvo, Arhiv Republike Slovenije, 2006.

Plutarch. *Plutarch's Lives: The Translation Called Dryden's*. 5 vols. Corrected from the Greek and revised by A. H. Clough. Boston: Little, Brown, 1906.

Posamentier, Alfred S., and Ingmar Lehmann. *A Biography of the World's Most Mysterious Number*. New York: Prometheus Books, 2004.

Sandifer, Edward. "Why 140 Digits of Pi Matter." In *Jurij Baron Vega in Njegov Čas: Zbornik Ob 250-Letnici Rojstva* [Baron Jurij Vega and his times: Celebrating 250 years], edited by Tomaž Pisanski et al., 240–254. Ljubljana: DMFA—založništvo, Arhiv Republike Slovenije, 2006.

Thomas, Ivor. *Greek Mathematical Works: Aristarchus to Pappus*. Vol. 2. Cambridge, MA: Loeb Classical Library, Harvard University Press, 1941.

Žargi, Matija. "The Heritage of Vega's Time." In *Jurij Baron Vega in Njegov Čas: Zbornik Ob 250-Letnici Rojstva* [Baron Jurij Vega and his times: Celebrating 250 years], edited by Tomaž Pisanski et al., 76–102. Ljubljana: DMFA—založništvo, Arhiv Republike Slovenije, 2006.

"The Queen's Chemise: Élisabeth Vigée Le Brun, Portraitist of Marie Antoinette" by Susan Campbell Bartoletti

Ashelford, Jane. "'Colonial Livery' and the *Chemise à la Reine*, 1779–1784." *Costume: Journal of the Costume Society* 52, no. 2 (2018): 217–239.

Covington, Richard. "Marie Antoinette." *Smithsonian Magazine*, November 2006. www.smithsonianmag.com/history/marie-antoinette-134629573/.

Diderot, Denis. *Essais sur la peinture*. Paris: François Buisson, 1795. https://archive.org/details/gri_000033125010886956/page/n89.

Fauveau, Auguste François, marquis de Frénilly. *Recollections of Baron de Frénilly: Peer of France (1768–1828)*. Edited by Arthur Chuquet. Translated by Frederic Lees. New York: G. P. Putnam's Sons, 1909.

Fried, Michael. *Absorption and Theatricality: Painting and Beholder in the Age of Diderot*. Chicago: University of Chicago Press, 1980.

Higonnet, Anne. "A True Revolutionary." *Apollo* 183, no. 640 (March 2016): 154–159.

May, Gita. *Elisabeth Vigée Le Brun: The Odyssey of an Artist in an Age of Revolution.* New Haven, CT: Yale University Press, 2005.

Sheriff, Mary D. *The Exceptional Woman: Elisabeth Vigée-Lebrun and the Cultural Politics of Art.* Chicago: University of Chicago Press, 1996.

Vigée Lebrun, Marie Louise Élisabeth. *Memoirs of Madame Vigée Lebrun.* Translated by Lionel Strachey. New York: Doubleday, Page & Co., 1903.

Woodward, Servanne. *Explorations de l'imaginaire de la représentation au dix-huitième siècle Français: Chardin, Vigée-Lebrun, Diderot, Marivaux.* Lewiston, NY: Edwin Mellen Press, 2001.

Zaleski, Erin. "The Scandalous Life of Marie Antoinette's Versailles Apartments." *The Daily Beast*, May 4, 2019. www.thedailybeast.com/the-scandalous-life-of-marie-antoinettes-versailles-apartments.

"The Choice: Paris, 1789" by Marc Aronson

Adams, William Howard. *The Paris Years of Thomas Jefferson.* New Haven, CT: Yale University Press, 1997.

Ellis, Joseph J. *American Sphinx: The Character of Thomas Jefferson.* New York: Knopf, 1997.

Ferling, John. *Apostles of Revolution: Jefferson, Paine, Monroe and the Struggle Against the Old Order in America and Europe.* New York: Bloomsbury, 2018.

———. *Setting the World Ablaze: Washington, Adams, Jefferson, and the American Revolution.* Oxford: Oxford University Press, 2000.

"From Thomas Jefferson to Maria Cosway, 12 October 1786," Founders Online, National Archives and Records Administration. Accessed October 4, 2019. https://founders.archives.gov/documents/Jefferson/01-10-02-0309.

Gordon-Reed, Annette. *The Hemingses of Monticello: An American Family.* New York: W. W. Norton, 2008.

Gordon-Reed, Annette, and Peter S. Onuf. *"Most Blessed of the Patriarchs": Thomas Jefferson and the Empire of the Imagination.* New York: Liveright, 2016.

Halliday, E. M. *Understanding Thomas Jefferson.* New York: HarperCollins, 2001.

Malone, Dumas. *Jefferson and the Rights of Man*. Boston: Little, Brown, 1951.

O'Brien, Conor Cruise. *The Long Affair: Thomas Jefferson and the French Revolution, 1785–1800*. Chicago: University of Chicago Press, 1996.

"'All Men Are Created Equal': The Global Journey of Olaudah Equiano" by Joyce Hansen

Bontemps, Arna, ed. *Great Slave Narratives*. Boston: Beacon Press, 1969.

Davis, Charles T. "The Slave Narrative: First Major Art Form in an Emerging Black Tradition." In *Black Is the Color of the Cosmos: Essays on Afro-American Literature and Culture, 1942–1981*. Edited by Charles T. Davis and Henry Louis Gates Jr. Washington, DC: Howard University Press, 1982.

Equiano, Olaudah. *The Interesting Narrative of the Life of Olaudah Equiano, or Gustavus Vassa, the African, Written by Himself.* Edited by Werner Sollors. New York: W. W. Norton, 2001.

Franklin, John Hope. *From Slavery to Freedom: A History of African Americans*. New York: Knopf, 2000.

"The Wesleyans in the West Indies" by Summer Edward

Aymer, Paula L. *Evangelical Awakenings in the Anglophone Caribbean: Studies from Grenada and Barbados*. New York: Palgrave Macmillan, 2016.

Beasley, Nicholas M. *Christian Ritual and the Creation of British Slave Societies, 1650–1780*. Athens: University of Georgia Press, 2009.

Bourne, George. *Slavery Illustrated in Its Effects Upon Woman and Domestic Society.* Boston: Isaac Knapp, 1837.

Coke, Thomas. *Extracts of the Journals of the Late Rev. Thomas Coke, L. L. D.; Comprising Several Visits to North America and the West-Indies: His Tour Through a Part of Ireland, and His Nearly Finished Voyage to Bombay in the East-Indies: To Which Is Prefixed, A Life of the Doctor.* Dublin: R. Napper, 1816.

———. *A History of the West Indies, Containing the Natural, Civil, and Ecclesiastical History of Each Island: With an Account of the Missions Instituted in Those Islands, from the Commencement of Their Civilization; but More Especially of the Missions Which Have Been Established in That Archipelago by the Society Late in Connexion with the Rev. John Wesley.* 3 vols. Vol. 1. Liverpool: Printed for the Author, 1808.

Duncan, Peter. *A Narrative of the Wesleyan Mission to Jamaica; with Occasional Remarks on the State of Society in That Colony.* London: Partridge and Oakey, 1849.

Equiano, Olaudah. "Miscellaneous Verses; or, Reflections on the State of My Mind." In *The Poetry of Slavery: An Anglo-American Anthology, 1764–1865*, edited by Marcus Wood, 150–153. Oxford: Oxford University Press, 2003.

Findlay, G. G., and W. W. Holdsworth. *The History of the Wesleyan Methodist Missionary Society.* 5 vols. Vol. 2. London: Epworth Press, 1921.

Finkelman, Paul, ed. *Encyclopedia of African American History, 1619–1895: From the Colonial Period to the Age of Frederick Douglass.* Oxford: Oxford University Press, 2006.

Goveia, Elsa V. *Slave Society in the British Leeward Islands at the End of the Eighteenth Century.* New Haven, CT: Yale University Press, 1965.

Matthews, Gelien. *Caribbean Slave Revolts and the British Abolitionist Movement.* Baton Rouge: Louisiana State University Press, 2006.

Misra, Anil Dutt. *Inspiring Thoughts of Mahatma Gandhi.* New Delhi: Concept Publishing, 2008.

Norris, Clive Murray. *The Financing of John Wesley's Methodism, c. 1740–1800.* Oxford: Oxford University Press, 2017.

Prince, Mary. *The History of Mary Prince, a West Indian Slave. Related by Herself. With a Supplement by the Editor. To Which Is Added, the Narrative of Asa-Asa, a Captured African.* Edited by Thomas Pringle. London: F. Westley and A. H. Davis, 1831.

Sergeant, Richard. *Letters from Jamaica on Subjects Historical, Natural and Religious.* London: John Mason, 1843.

Sinha, Manisha. *The Slave's Cause: A History of Abolition.* New Haven, CT: Yale University Press, 2016.

Watson, Richard. *A Defence of the Wesleyan Methodist Missions in the West Indies: Including a Refutation of the Charges in Mr. Marryat's "Thoughts on the Abolition of the Slave Trade, &c." and in Other Publications; with Facts and Anecdotes Illustrative of the Moral State of the Slaves, and of the Operation of Missions.* London: T. Cordeux, 1817.

Wesley, John. "Farther Thoughts on Separation from the Church." In *The Miscellaneous Works of the Rev. John Wesley.* 3 vols. Vol. 3. New York: J. & J. Harper, 1828.

——. *The Journal of the Reverend John Wesley, A. M., Sometime Fellow of Lincoln College, Oxford.* 2 vols. Vol. 1. New York: T. Mason and G. Lane, 1837.

——. "Predestination Calmly Considered." In *The Works of John Wesley.* Vol. 10. London: Wesleyan Conference Office, 1872; repr., Grand Rapids, MI: Zondervan, 1958.

——. *The Works of the Rev. John Wesley.* Vol. 1: *An Account of His Family; of His Education in the Early Part of His Life, and the First Five Numbers of His Journal.* New York: J. & J. Harper, 1827.

——. *The Works of the Rev. John Wesley, A.M.* New York: Carlton & Porter, 1831.

Wesley, John, and Charles Wesley. *Reasons Against a Separation from the Church of England: With Hymns for the Preachers among the Methodists (So Called).* London: W. Strahan, 1760.

"Who Counted in America? The Beginning of an Endless Conversation"
by Cynthia Levinson and Sanford Levinson

"An act to establish an uniform Rule of Naturalization" (March 26, 1790). Accessed January 22, 2020. https://immigrationhistory.org/item/1790-nationality-act/.

Beeman, Richard R. *Plain, Honest Men: The Making of the American Constitution.* New York: Random House, 2009.

Berkin, Carol. *A Sovereign People: The Crises of the 1790s and the Birth of American Nationalism.* New York: Basic Books, 2017.

Bordewich, Fergus M. *The First Congress: How James Madison, George Washington, and a Group of Extraordinary Men Invented the Government.* New York: Simon & Schuster, 2016.

Davidson, James West, William E. Gienapp, Christine Leigh Heyrman, Mark H. Lytle, and Michael B. Stoff. *Nation of Nations: A Narrative History of the American Republic.* 5th ed. Boston: McGraw Hill, 2005.

Debates in House of Representatives. August 17, 1789. In *Documentary History of the First Federal Congress, 1789–1791.* Baltimore: Johns Hopkins University Press, 1972–2017.

"Declaration of the Rights of Man—1789." Avalon Project, Yale Law School. Accessed October 1, 2019. http://avalon.law.yale.edu/18th_century/rightsof.asp.

The Federalist Papers, No. 15. Avalon Project, Yale Law School. Accessed October 1, 2019. https://avalon.law.yale.edu/18th_century/fed15.asp.

The Federalist Papers, No. 48. Avalon Project, Yale Law School. Accessed October 1, 2019. https://avalon.law.yale.edu/18th_century/fed48.asp.

Maclay, William. *Journal of William Maclay: United States Senator from Pennsylvania, 1789–1791*. Edited by Edgar S. Maclay. New York: D. Appleton and Company, 1890. Accessed October 1, 2019. https://archive.org/stream /journalwilliamm01maclgoog#page/n188/mode/2up. PDF/Epub.

191st Court of the Commonwealth of Massachusetts. General Laws. Section 36: Blasphemy. Accessed October 1, 2019. https://malegislature.gov/Laws /GeneralLaws/PartIV/TitleI/Chapter272/Section36.

Raphael, Ray. *Mr. President: How and Why the Founders Created a Chief Executive.* New York: Vintage Books, 2012.

Remini, Robert V. *The House: The History of the House of Representatives*. New York: HarperCollins, 2006.

"Mary Jemison and the Seneca Nation: 1789" by Christopher Turner

Hauptman, Laurence M. *Coming Full Circle: The Seneca Nation of Indians, 1848–1934*. Norman: University of Oklahoma Press, 2019.

Horsman, Reginald. *Expansion and American Indian Policy, 1783–1812.* East Lansing: Michigan State University Press, 1967.

Jennings, Francis. "The Constitutional Evolution of the Covenant Chain." *Proceedings of the American Philosophical Society* 115, no. 2 (April 22, 1971): 88–96.

Johansen, Bruce Elliott, and Barbara Alice Mann, eds. *Encyclopedia of the Haudenosaunee (Iroquois Confederacy)*. Westport, CT: Greenwood Press, 2000.

The Journals of the Continental Congress, 1774–1789. Vol. 34. Washington, DC: Library of Congress, 1904–1937.

Mann, Barbara Alice. *George Washington's War on Native America.* Westport, CT: Praeger, 2005.

Prucha, Francis Paul. *The Great Father: The United States Government and the American Indians.* Lincoln: University of Nebraska Press, 1984.

Seaver, James E. *A Narrative of the Life of Mrs. Mary Jemison.* Edited by June Namias. Norman: University of Oklahoma Press, 1995.

"Challenging Time: Dr. James Hutton, the Father of Geology" by Sally M. Walker

Gould, Stephen Jay. "Fall in the House of Ussher." *Natural History* 100 (November 1991): 12–21.

Hutton, James. "Theory of the Earth; or, An Investigation of the Laws Observable in the Composition, Dissolution, and Restoration of Land upon the Globe." *Transactions of the Royal Society of Edinburgh* 1 (1788).

———. *Theory of the Earth: With Proofs and Illustrations.* Vol. 1. Weinheim, Germany: H. R. Engelmann (J. Cramer), 1959.

Jones, Jean. "The Geological Collection of James Hutton." *Annals of Science* 41, no. 3 (1984).

Jones, Jean, Hugh S. Torrens, and Eric Robinson. "The Correspondence between James Hutton (1726–1797) and James Watt (1736–1819) with Two Letters from Hutton to George Clerk-Maxwell (1715–1784): Part 1." *Annals of Science* 51, no. 6 (1994).

Playfair, John. "Biographical Account of the Late Dr. James Hutton." *Transactions of the Royal Society of Edinburgh* 5 (1805).

Repcheck, Jack. *The Man Who Found Time: James Hutton and the Discovery of the Earth's Antiquity.* Cambridge, MA: Perseus, 2003.

"Mutiny on the *Bounty*: Breadfruit, Flogging, Impossible Navigation, and Revolutionary Ideas—There Ought to Be a Musical" by Steve Sheinkin

Alexander, Caroline. *The Bounty: The True Story of the Mutiny on the* Bounty. New York: Viking, 2003.

Barrow, John. *The Eventful History of the Mutiny and Piratical Seizure of H.M.S.* Bounty: *Its Cause and Consequences.* London: John Murray, 1831.

Bligh, William. *The Mutiny on Board H.M.S.* Bounty. New York: Airmont Publishing, 1965.

Bligh, William, and Edward Christian. *The* Bounty *Mutiny.* New York: Penguin, 2001.

Hough, Richard. *Captain Bligh and Mr. Christian: The Men and the Mutiny.* New York: E. P. Dutton, 1973.

McKinney, Sam. *Bligh: A True Account of Mutiny Aboard His Majesty's Ship* Bounty. Camden, ME: International Marine Publishing, 1989.

Morrison, James. *After the* Bounty: *A Sailor's Account of the Mutiny, and Life in the South Seas.* Edited by Donald A. Maxton. Washington, DC: Potomac Books, 2010.

Rupp, Rebecca. "Breadfruit and 'The Bounty' That Brought It Across the Ocean." *National Geographic*, April 28, 2016.

Tagart, Edward. *A Memoir of the Late Captain Peter Heywood, R. N. With Extracts from His Diaries and Correspondence.* London: Effingham Wilson, 1832.

INDEX